*How did a black kid from Massachusetts
come to head the nation's medical schools?*

*How did a cash-strapped average medical school move
into the top tier of research institutions?*

WILSON'S WAY
WIN, DON'T WHINE

A Minority Medical Leader's Relentless Rise to the Top

By
Donald E. Wilson, MD, MACP
With
Cindy S. Spitzer

Copyright 2009 Donald E. Wilson and Cindy S. Spitzer
All rights reserved.

ISBN: 1-4392-2268-1
ISBN-13: 9781439222683

Visit www.booksurge.com to order additional copies.

In memory of my mother, father and sister who always provided me with a stable family and taught me that hard work is itself a reward.

I dedicate this book to my wife Patricia Cela Littell. Her support of me has been unwavering, even when I was wrong. And she never whined.

Donald E. Wilson, MD, MACP

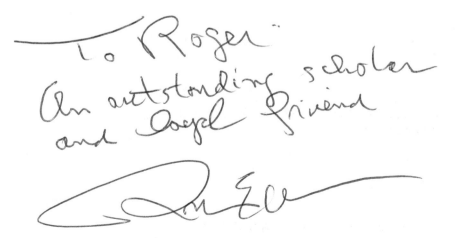

ACKNOWLEDGEMENTS

I humbly acknowledge my friend the late J. Tyson Tildon, Ph.D. who initially encouraged me to write this book.

I would like to thank everyone who patiently gave of his/her time to be interviewed for this book.

I especially thank Jeanette Balotin, my former chief of staff, whose advice and persistence made this book possible.

Donald E. Wilson, MD, MACP

TABLE OF CONTENTS

Introduction, part 1 –
Why I Almost Couldn't Write This Book   i
        by Cindy S. Spitzer

Introduction, part 2 –
Why I Let Them Talk Me into This Book   v
        by Donald E. Wilson, MD

Chapter 1   Wilson Who?   1
    Who is Donald Wilson and Why Should I Care?

Chapter 2   Pennies From Heaven   7
    Mighty Fine Grades… for a Colored Boy

Chapter 3   Becoming Doctor Wilson   29
    Smart, Black, and on Track

Chapter 4   Heeding the Call of Academic Medicine   53
    Blazing a Trail Less Traveled

Chapter 5   Maryland Meets Its Match   83
    First African-American Dean of a Predominantly White Medical School

Chapter 6   A Different Kind of Dean   99
   Less Like the Chairman of the Board,
   More Like the CEO

Chapter 7   C – Changes   119
   Transforming the Curriculum and the Culture

Chapter 8   The Wilson Effect   149
   Think Big, Deliver Bigger

Chapter 9   Wilson's Words to the Wise   169
   Seven Suggestions for Deans and Other Leaders

Chapter 10 Wilson's Way: Win, Don't Whine   199
   Ten Success Secrets for Everyone, Everywhere

INTRODUCTION, PART 1

Why I Almost Couldn't Write This Book
by Cindy S. Spitzer

I am a writer who enjoys blowing someone else's horn. To tell the story of someone as brilliant, bold, and accomplished as Dr. Donald E. Wilson is my idea of heaven on earth. Except when it's a living hell.

Let me explain.

Imagine, if you will, that you have just been introduced to a man whose bold vision and uncompromising leadership have transformed the nation's oldest public medical school from a previously ho-hum institution to one of the top medical schools in the country. Actually, for many of you, you *have* just been introduced.

Now imagine that this powerful, articulate, and tremendously accomplished man, who wishes you to write his book in a timely manner, doesn't want to talk too much about the difficulties he faced in his life *or* how he solved these problems. In addition to his deep reluctance to dwell on the negative or brag about the positive, this highly rational and efficient man is also not especially interested in revealing his personal feelings or spending too much time analyzing exactly what he did or why he did it.

For example, he doesn't really know *why* he decided, so completely and so irrevocably at the tender age of nine, to become a doctor, and frankly, he's getting sick and tired of you asking about it. Nor does he think it's any big deal that, as the first person in his family to ever go to college, he graduated with honors from Harvard College. And he doesn't particularly want to talk at great length about how, in less than a decade, he managed to turn the University of Maryland School of Medicine into a force to be reckoned with, despite deep budget cuts, mediocre facilities, outdated practices, and the occasionally mutinous department chair.

The plain truth is, this very busy and most accomplished gentleman doesn't particularly want to talk to you *at all*. He's got work to do.

So you hunt around, here and there. You interview all kinds of people, pour over various newspaper clippings, and wade through stacks of meeting notes, school documents, and transcripts of his many award acceptance speeches (he wins dozens). On occasion, you even get to annoy him in person with your repetitive questions about how it is that he ended up in this big, leather-bound office on the 14th floor of the University of Maryland medical school. That is, if you are lucky enough to get an appointment.

You gather and knit together the various threads of the story, and slowly it begins to dawn on you that this large, well-dressed man with the big gold ring and the countless awards, who reluctantly reveals bits and pieces of his life in his stately office on the 14th floor, is *truly brilliant*. Not just a highly capable and dynamic leader, not merely a really smart guy with a photographic memory and a non-stop work ethic, like a beaver tackling Niagara Falls, but a truly brilliant individual with a mind as luminous as a white-hot super nova.

And oh, did I mention that he's black?

With that entire in mind, now imagine that this brilliant person, who has asked you to write his story, without actually *giving* you much of the story, also doesn't particularly want to you to dwell on the fact that he is an African-American. He'd just as soon you not make too big a deal about the time when in 1966 the Air Force sent him to Nebraska to become Chief of Internal Medicine and Chairman of the Department of Medicine at the base hospital, and the local white landlords refused to rent him an apartment. Or the fact that, even right here in Baltimore, when he's not wearing his white doctor's coat, Wilson is sometimes followed by security guards in department stores and may have difficulty finding a cab driver willing to pick him up off the street.

Not that he's unaware that racism has to go *somewhere* in the book.

"Maybe just stick it in a chapter at the end," he suggests offhandedly as he reads through his mail.

Yeah, right.

I am not indulging in hyperbole when I assert that, even without the accolade of "the first black dean of a majority medical school" trailing after his name into eternity, Donald E. Wilson is easily one of the nation's top academic leaders of all time. Here is a man who excelled, not just in one career, but throughout his lifetime: first as an accomplished gastrointestinal physician, then as one of the world's leading experts on prostaglandins, and finally as the dynamic dean-turned-CEO who transformed the University of Maryland medical school into a powerhouse of research and cutting edge clinical care. Under Dr. Wilson's firm leadership, revenues to the medical school didn't just increase, they *quadrupled,* skyrocketing the school to the top of the charts. Most deans barely make it four years before moving on to other positions. Donald Wilson, on the other hand, has given the University of Maryland fifteen years of relentless, often eighty hours a week of nearly non-stop service. Translated into mere human terms, that comes to more than twenty-five years of average deanship in fifteen years. Certainly, this truly phenomenal individual needn't be black, too, to make this one heck of a compelling story.

But I could no more have left racism to the end of Dr. Wilson's book than he could have left it to the end of his life. While certainly not the whole story, the obstacles of racism have been ever-present through all his accomplishments, despite his firm determination and keen ability to function as if they weren't. My problem was *not* that I was a white woman writing about a black man. (Actually, that was easier than you might think). The problem was getting it on paper in a way that would simultaneously satisfy my drive to tell you all about it, while satisfying his desire not to dwell on it too much.

The terrible truth is that, for far longer than I am willing to admit, I hopelessly struggled with this book. Not because there wasn't enough to tell, but because there was so much to tell and yet he himself seemed so reluctant to tell it. In fact, I floundered with it for so long, it's a miracle I wasn't fired.

And then it dawned on me.

The more I learned about Dr. Wilson's life and accomplishments, the more I realized that the difficulties I thought I faced in telling his story were really not obstacles at all. As he himself has demonstrated, time and again, a challenge is nothing more than an opportunity to surprise someone—maybe even yourself.

So, how do you write a book about a brilliant man who refuses to blow his own horn? You blow it for him. I only hope Dr. Wilson's story inspires you half as much as it has me.

Cindy Spitzer

Baltimore, MD
November 2008

INTRODUCTION, PART 2

Why I Let Them Talk Me into This Book
by Donald E. Wilson, MD

I am not a man who enjoys eulogizing me, which is why when some of my colleagues started talking to me about this book I was less than enthusiastic. As dean of the University of Maryland School of Medicine, I didn't have time to write a book, and frankly, I really didn't want to.

But there is a good deal more to being dean than doing only what one might like. Early on in my career, I came to realize that my life is not strictly about what I hope to achieve for myself and my family, but also about what I might accomplish for others, be they patients, medical students, fellow physicians, or those who may follow me into academic medicine.

As a young man at Harvard University and Tufts University Medical School in the 1950s and early 1960s, I never saw a single African-American professor. As an eager resident at Boston's VA Hospital in the mid-1960s, I never saw a single African-American physician. And prior to coming to the University of Maryland in 1991 to lead the School of Medicine, I never saw a single African-American dean of a majority medical school—at least not until I looked in a mirror and saw myself.

Even today, half a century since the landmark *Brown vs. the Board of Education* Supreme Court decision opened the door to equal education for all students, only about 4.4 percent of the nation's 725,000 physicians are African-American. Less than 1 percent of the leaders of our 100,000 academic medical faculty are people of color. And while four black men have served with distinction as deans of majority medical schools since my appointment in 1991, as of the date of my retirement on September 1, 2006 there was still only a single permanent black dean of a majority medical school in our nation.

Clearly, that needs to change.

The change I'm talking about will not happen automatically, like winter melting into spring. It takes the on-going work of many people, in countless big and small ways. It takes the work of medical school physicians and faculty who are dedicated to attracting, retaining, and mentoring underrepresented minority medical students. It takes medical school administrators who are sensitive to the subtle and not-so-subtle racial barriers that still exist, despite years of affirmative action and now the rising tide of anti-affirmative action sentiment. And it takes a willingness to go beyond the daily business of growing and running a medical school to do a few things that one might just as soon not do—like writing a book.

So I agreed to let my late friend and colleague Tyson Tilden, PhD, and my then-chief of staff, Jeanette Balotin, find a writer to tackle my biography. The task was handed to award-winning writer Cindy Spitzer, who despite taking much longer than anyone had hoped to get the job done, and despite being a white woman with no experience in academic medicine, has somehow managed to capture the essence of my life and times.

My hope is this book will provide a look at what a medical school dean actually does for a living, a topic conspicuously missing from the scientific literature. I would also be delighted if the book encourages young people, especially young African-Americans, to think beyond society's expectations and give serious consideration to choosing careers

Introduction, Part 2

in medicine, especially academic medicine. It really is quite a wonderful and rewarding profession—and we desperately need them.

Some people may feel that the book unnecessarily dwells on race. The plain truth is that we are all living in a white man's world, so we might as well learn to make the best of it. Regardless of your field of interest, if you are an African American or any under-represented minority you needn't take on other people's expectations of you, nor let other people set your goals. You can decide for yourself what *you* want and then work hard to make it happen. Find realistic ways to turn the negatives into positives, and work to lift yourself and those around you along the way.

Although this book pertains directly to medical school deans, it also applies to anyone in a position of leadership, or to anyone who wishes to be. Whether you are (or aspire to be) the dean of an academic institution, a corporate CEO, a politician, a religious or community leader, or the head of any group or organization, you can win and achieve your goals no matter your race or gender.

Regardless of your career path, I hope this book will inspire readers from all walks of life to understand that, although the world will no doubt throw a lot of crap your way, you too can defy expectations. Perhaps even your own.

Donald E. Wilson, MD, MACP

Baltimore, Maryland
November 2008

CHAPTER 1

Wilson Who?
Who is Donald Wilson and Why Should I Care?

Who decides how far you can and cannot go in your life? Your family? Your education? The color of your skin? The expectations of your culture?

Certainly, one's upbringing, education, and place in society all leave their mark, and sometimes take their toll. And clearly, basic intelligence, along with mental and physical health also impact your opportunities and choices.

But what *really* makes someone get up every morning and take the high road or the low, or more often, the path of least resistance? Why do most of us just roll along with whatever comes our way, while another man stretches himself beyond all expectations, not just for a few productive years, but relentlessly and without compromise for an entire lifetime?

Donald Edward Wilson is one such man.

You may not have heard his name before, but listen for a moment to what others have said about him:

Dr. Wilson is not just a brilliant guy, he's like a bulldozer who won't stop until he gets the job done, no matter what gets in his way. And yet somehow, no one gets hurt. He's really a very decent, very brilliant guy.

Dr. Freeman Hrabowski
President
University of Maryland Baltimore County

There are two sides to this man. He can be fired up, passionate, and as persistent as anyone I've ever met. But he is so modest that when he has to accept an award (and he wins an awful lot of them), you almost feel sorry for him.

Dr. Jessie Harris
Dean of the University of Maryland School of Social Work

Don Wilson simply exudes collaboration and humility. He's smart, honest and efficient. He cuts through all the BS and yet he pulls you in. There's no glitter, no hype; it's all quality. No matter how you measure it, Don Wilson is simply the best medical school dean in modern history. It's been an honor to know him.

Richard Taylor, MD
Former President, University of Maryland Medical Alumni Association

Wilson Who?

No, this is not a story about some saint. What good would that do us? This is the story of a real man who, when given the chance, squeezed all he could out of every opportunity. And when not given the chance, he squeezed all he could out of himself.

Few people, beyond his immediate family in Worcester, MA, expected any of it. The son of a hard-working, fiercely independent father and a softhearted, nurturing mother, Donald learned quite early in life to read and write, and was soon bringing home what school teachers back in the 1940s called "mighty fine grades—for a colored boy."

At the end of sixth grade, the white principal, looking out for what he assumed was in Donald's best interest, advised his parents to send their bright-eyed son to the town's vocational school where most of the town's African-American boys went to learn a trade. Sensing resistance, Donald's principal sincerely warned his parents to be "realistic" about their son's options. "You've got to think about the boy's future."

And right then and there, that could have been the end of it. At age twelve, Donald Wilson, like so many other capable boys of color in 1948, could have gone on to the local trade school to become an auto mechanic, a pipe fitter, or a janitor. A damn good auto mechanic, pipe fitter, or janitor, to be sure, but that could easily have been the end of the line for him.

Instead, Donald's parents, who never even graduated grade school, had an entirely different vision for their brilliant son.

"No," his father said flatly, despite the principal's fierce objections. "Donald is going to Dix Street Preparatory school, like all the other smart kids. No good reason in this whole wide world he can't."

Even in hindsight, it's hard to pinpoint the exact moment one steps onto The Path. Certainly, no matter what course you take in life, there are countless side trails that lead to no place special. But for Donald Wilson, once his father set him upon the track to attend the totally white prep school and then move on to the mostly white, college-bound North High School, there would be no derailment, no turning back.

For him, showing up on that first day of class with his pencils cleanly sharpened and his mind hungry for work, Donald stepped onto a path that led to a highway of future opportunities and choices. At any point along the way he could have allowed himself to simply slow down, pull over, and set up camp. Instead, Wilson drove himself relentlessly to the tops of mountains and discovered he could fly.

He's the boldest leader I have ever known. If you want to know a real leader, look at who's following him.

Carol Boyer
Former assistant to a former University of Maryland president

He was the right man at the right time.

Barbara Heller
Former dean of the University of Maryland School of Nursing

He's a force to be reckoned with. A brilliant, accomplished man.

Otha Miles, MD
University of Maryland School of Medicine alumnus

Wilson Who?

But you needn't take their word for it. Come see for yourself.

To the extent you can measure a man by the sheer weight of his Curriculum Vitae, Donald E. Wilson's CV spans an astonishing thirty-four pages. Highlights include:

- Harvard University and Tufts University Medical School
- 8 Hospital Appointments
- 6 Faculty Appointments
- 160 Published Original Scientific Papers and Abstracts
- Editor of 5 journals
- 120 Scientific Research Presentations in 8 countries
- Medical Licenses in 6 states
- 2 years of military medical service
- Chaired 22 Scientific and Medical Meetings (Not attended, *chaired*.)
- Member and/or chair of 11 federal scientific committees for the NIH, FDA, and DHHS
- 48 scientific and medical society memberships
- 18 hospital and non-hospital board memberships
- Master of the American College of Physicians – an honor bestowed on less than 1 percent of its members
- Member of the Institute of Medicine, National Academy of Sciences
- "The Nation's Dean" – Chairman of the Council of Deans of the Association of American Medical Colleges
- Chairman of the Association of American Medical Colleges
- Chairman, Maryland Health Care Access and Cost Commission and Maryland Health Care Commission
- Vice Chairman, Prince George's County Hospital Authority
- And more than 60 other Honors, Awards, and Special Appointments

Now, take a look at what the University of Maryland School of Medicine has managed to achieve—despite an almost nonstop barrage of budget cuts, political upheaval, entrenched power struggles, and countless near catastrophes of every description—since Don Wilson firmly took the helm:

- Total revenues to the school *quadrupled* since 1991
- State-of-the-art research facilities expanded to nearly *half a million* square feet
- Four new departments, six organized research centers, and five new programs added
- Number of under-represented minority faculty quadrupled
- First medical school to require laptop computers for students
- Curriculum entirely revamped to include interactive learning, holistic treatment, and cutting-edge information technologies
- University of Maryland School of Medicine climbed up from the third quartile of all medical schools in research funding in 1991, to the top quartile in 2005 with more than a quadrupling of research funds.

These lists may read like a Hollywood fantasy, but in fact it's all true and more. So I ask you, is it possible that Donald Wilson can tell us something about what we can and cannot do with our lives?

Come along with me now and we'll go for a walk down *Wilson's Way*.

CHAPTER 2

Pennies From Heaven
Mighty Fine Grades... for a Colored Boy

Every time it rains, it rains pennies from heaven.
Don't you know each cloud contains pennies from heaven?
You'll find your fortune falling all over town.
Be sure your umbrella is upside down.
Trade them for a package of sunshine and flowers.
If you want the things you love, you must have showers.
So when you hear it thunder, don't run under a tree.
There'll be pennies from heaven for you and me.
"Pennies From Heaven"
By Arthur Johnston and John Burk

Just days after Bing Crosby first recorded the 1936 hit song *Pennies from Heaven*, Donald Edward Wilson was born on August 28 in the New England town of Worcester, Massachusetts.

1936 was the year that president Franklin Delano Roosevelt won in a landslide his second of four terms in the White House, and the year that Congress passed a law banning child labor, as well as requiring a minimum wage and a forty-hour work week for companies with government contracts. 1936 was also the year Bennie Goodman first integrated his all-white orchestra by hiring African-American pianist Teddy Wilson and vibraphonist Lionel Hampton. It was the year that Orson Wells directed the first all-black cast of Macbeth. And the year that track and field star Jesse Owens competed in the 1936 Summer Olympics in Berlin, Germany, becoming the first African-America athlete to come home a hero with four gold medals. The world into which Donald was born was, indeed, changing.

But not very quickly.

Just a few years before Donald's birth, his young father ran for his life, forced to leave his new wife and extended family in South Carolina to avoid being lynched.

> *I never really knew the whole story. It was described to me as "to escape a lynching" and that to me meant to escape his lynching. My guess is, my father—and I'm pretty much like my father—didn't let people say things to him he didn't like. My father could be very vocal about what he thought. In those days, when talking to a white person, you couldn't look directly at them. You couldn't look them right in the eyes. You always had to look down at your feet when you were talking to a white person.*

So twenty-year-old Rivers Wilson fled north to the small Hudson River village of Tarrytown, New York, where he earned what little he could working for the rail road, stashing a few coins each week in an old jelly jar.

Just pennies, really. But pennies add up.

In time, Rivers saved enough to move even further north, to Massachusetts. Not long after, he emptied his jar again and sent what little he had back down South so his fifteen-year-old wife, Licine, could join him. There, the two young newly weds settled into the quiet working-class town of Worcester, where the old mills had already shut down and a few factories would later make guns and airplane parts for the war effort. Licine did what she could to make them a home, and Rivers did what he could to add a few more pennies to the jelly jar. Donald's father never liked the idea of working for someone else and finding work wasn't easy, so he decided to be his own boss and set out to build himself a business hauling trash.

Now that's *trash*, mind you, not garbage. There is a distinction. Back then, the town of Worcester was responsible for picking up the "garbage," meaning anything that could be sold to hog farmers to feed to their pigs. That left all the rest of folk's "trash"—tons of coal ashes, tin cans, pieces of wood, broken glass, bits of metal, and all manner of other junk—to be hauled away by a dozen or so local entrepreneurs with trucks, who charged a small fee to pick up, sort, and drag the stuff off to the town's incinerator or dump, depending on the what they got.

Each bit of trash paid only pennies, but pennies add up. Soon, the old jelly jar of coins gave way to paper envelopes bulging with folding money. A few dollars went into the Food Envelope, a couple more were stashed into the House Envelope, and so on. Rivers liked the idea of working on his own and earning what he could, with no one to hold him back or control his fate.

> *"No matter what you do in life," my father would tell me again and again, "you don't want to have a job where you work for somebody else." Being colored, he said, meant you'd have to be "twice as good as everyone else to do just as well—and even that might not be good enough."*

Rivers had himself a truck and hauling trash seemed as good a way as any to keep his destiny out of other people's hands. He had himself a truck—and he had Donald.

Even as a child, Donald was a sturdy boy with a strong back, nimble hands, and a quick mind eager to learn. As soon as he was old enough to scoop a bit of trash into a bucket, Donald worked right along side his father, hauling filthy coal ashes out of people's homes. At age eight, when he could finally see over the top of the truck's big steering wheel, the boy often drove his father's old dump truck as the two of them hauled trash for many hours after school. And when school was out during the steamy hot summer months, Donald and Rivers worked side by side, collecting, sorting, and hauling trash—not just for an hour or two, but for six grueling hours a day, six days a week, all summer long.

> *It was hard, boring, dirty work, but day in and day out, we got the job done. To haul trash, you had to go down into people's basements and shovel their coal ashes into a big canvas bag. Then you'd pull it up onto your back, walk it outside to the street, and dump it in the truck. Then you'd turn around and do it again and again. You had to carefully sort the stuff and then bring each item to the right place. If you brought the trash that shouldn't be burned to the incinerator or the trash that shouldn't be buried to the dump, you could be fined and you might not be able to go back there again. Hauling trash was hard work. I didn't particularly like it, but I did it and he paid me.*

Not that trash-hauling was all the family ever envisioned for him.

"I was ten when Donald was born," recalled sister Rena. "I went to the hospital and my mother asked me 'What should we name our fine boy?' I knew no one wanted any Juniors in the family, so I thought about it for a while and I said we should name him *Donald Edward Wilson*—just in case he goes off and becomes a doctor or something. We didn't know what he might do, but we knew it could be something big. He needed an important name."

Pennies From Heaven

Together, Rena, Donald, Rivers, and Licine made a good life for themselves in Worcester. In addition to the immediate family and a couple of cats named "Sir James" and "Foots," an assortment of relatives came, from time to time, to live at the Wilson home, including four cousins from Licine's side of the family. Despite the extra of mouths to feed and people to clothe, Rena remembers "We never wanted for anything. We always had plenty of food. If anyone came to the door around dinner time, my mother always fed them. We weren't rich, but we never felt poor one day of our lives."

Rivers hauled enough trash to support his family, pay a bit to his growing boy, and still put some money aside. Just pennies, really. But pennies add up.

Eventually, Rivers saved enough to buy a house, a "double-decker," meaning each of its two floors was a separate apartment. Donald's family lived on the top; his godmother rented the bottom. In time, Donald's father saved enough of that rent money to buy another double-decker, which he also rented out. Then he bought a triple-decker and rented out those three apartments, as well. Then another house and another. Eventually, he got himself an even bigger house with eight separate apartments. In time, Rivers Wilson owned ten houses—all completely his, all pulling in rent, all from hauling trash.

Rivers hauled trash every day, except Sundays when the family went to church. Sometimes, the whole family attended the Worcester John Street Baptist Church. More often, only Licine and the children went, while Rivers got caught up on other work. But no matter what else he had to do, every Sunday after church, Rivers took the family to the park. And later that same day, he would take Donald to town to see the local picture show.

> *I'm not even sure if he liked it, but we always went, just the two of us. Every Sunday, we'd walk together to the movie theater, about twenty minutes each way, and go inside and see two pictures, usually a Western and a serial, and then four cartoons. Afterwards, we'd always go across the street to a little hot dog place—three for a quarter. Then we'd walk home. To this day, I still love hot dogs.*

Back home, Donald's mother would fill the house with the irresistible smells of Sunday dinner: roast beef, leg of lamb, or fried chicken, along with freshly baked biscuits, green beans, corn, or whatever ripe vegetable was ready to be picked from the backyard garden that fed the family from May to September.

Part American Indian, part African American, Licine was what people called "a good Christian woman." As a southern girl who came North to join her husband, young Licine "went right to work cleaning houses on her hands and knees," recalls Rena. "All her money was used to support the family, while my father saved his money to buy the first property." After work, she would come home and cook and clean her own house.

Licine was soft-spoken, big-hearted, and as strong as nails when she needed to be. Once when Donald's father was under his trash truck, trying to fix something, the pick-up accidentally fell off the jack, pinning Rivers to the ground. Licine ran outside and single-handedly lifted up a corner of the truck while Donald's godmother ran for help.

When she wasn't cleaning, cooking, feeding people, and taking care of her family, Licine liked to sew, making dresses and shirts for the family. One time, she even made a classic Chesterfield coat after examining one carefully in a fancy store. Sunday mornings, when most stores in Worcester were closed for the day, Licine and the rest of the family would go to the Jewish section of town where the butcher shops stayed open. There, Licine would select lamb and veal roasts, chickens, fish, various cuts of beef, and whatever other meats the family needed for the week. Every day had its own special food: Friday nights they had fish, Saturday was franks and beans, and of course, Sunday was always a big spread. On the weekends, even breakfast was a feast: veal chops, grits, "salt fish," and more of Licine's homemade biscuits.

> *My mother could cook, and we could eat. There was always someone extra joining us for dinner—some relatives or neighbors or people from church. My mother would feed the whole world if she could.*

Donald's taste for his mother's home cooking was exceeded only by his appetite for knowledge. Donald learned to read at the age of three, and was soon devouring every book he could get. While Licine fed his body and soul and Rivers built his muscles and character, books gave Donald's hungry mind something more to chew on. When asked now about his favorite book and what kinds of topics he liked to read, Donald says: "I didn't read that much. I just liked to read everything I could."

Although neither of Donald's parents went to grammar school, they both had an abiding faith in the transformational power of education. Work, church, and family were important, but if their bright-eyed son was ever to make something of himself in this world, he was going to have to have good schooling. Donald's parents never pushed him to get good grades or to do his homework. They didn't have to. Learning just came easily to Donald, who as long as anyone can remember always had a keenly observant eye for detail and a nearly photographic memory.

Wilson's Way

Snooky. Donald's mutt from 1939–50; Worcester, MA

Donald age 4 with Snooky behind him. Worcester, MA 1940

"My brother was truly a brilliant child," recalled Rena. "He loved books, and he remembered each and everything he ever read or was taught. Even Sunday school lessons. He never had to study. He just remembered everything."

Like the pennies earned from hauling bits of trash, grains of knowledge earned everyday added up over time. But unlike money, which only diminishes when spent, knowledge becomes a lifetime investment that only grows more valuable with use. And even better, it can never be stolen, no matter what the world throws your way. Donald's father used to say, "The only thing no one can ever take away from you," my father used to tell me, "is your education."

But first, Donald would have to get one.

Like most New England towns in the 1940s, housing in Worcester was racially segregated along either side of the railroad tracks that ran north and south. Only about 1 percent of the families in Worcester were African-American, and about 90 percent of them lived on the East Side of the tracks. The rest, including Donald's family, lived on the West Side. There, Donald went to grammar school in a large class of mostly white children.

> *About eight or nine of the forty kids in my class were black, and the teacher just assumed we couldn't do very much. Up until the middle of the second grade, the teachers gave me C's in everything, except an A in what they called Effort and Conduct. Basically, if you were being a nice boy, if you didn't create any problems, if you kept your mouth shut and didn't talk in class, they gave you an A in Effort and Conduct. That was their way of saying the other C grades were the best I could do, that I was working at capacity, as a C-type person. The thing I find so interesting, in retrospect, is that they never even called on me to find out what I knew.*

But in the middle of second grade, Donald's family moved to a new school district and suddenly all that changed. After years of hauling trash and collecting rent on those double and triple-deckers, Rivers had found a $15,000 home he wanted to buy that happened to be in a white neighborhood, also on the West Side. Back then, banks would only lend money for the "right" home in the "right" part of town to the "right" person, so the seller naturally assumed Rivers would never get a mortgage. "That's OK," Donald's father assured the man. "I'll pay cash."

In his new school, Donald discovered that the teachers, many who had never taught a black student before, were free of preconceived expectations of what he could and couldn't do.

> *They didn't assume anything. They didn't have enough experience to stereotype me as being intellectually fallow. They just basically treated me like everybody else, and from that day on, my grades (except in penmanship) were all A's.*

Donald's formidable mind took in and assimilated ideas and information as effortlessly as most children consume candy. Everything in school was easy for him as he glided through his lessons, quickly completing his homework assignments and conquering his tests without much studying. Donald enjoyed his new school and made friends easily, although some not quite as easily as others.

> *There was this one kid who used to always call me "Sambo." I didn't like that. I was eight and Bruce was a half year older than me and the tallest kid in his class. I told him to stop calling me that. He didn't. So I beat the crap out of him. He was a lot bigger than me, but I had something he lacked: commitment. I never told anyone about the fight, but he did. After that, he never called me "Sambo" again, and neither did anyone else. It took awhile, but eventually Bruce became one of my very best friends at that school.*

"Donald was like that from the start," says sister Rena. "A wonderful, kind person, but not someone who would tolerate any garbage. One time, when Donald was just three or four years old, my mother heard our little dog yelp from another room. When we went in there, we discovered that Donald—who really loved animals—had just *bitten* the dog. My mother said, 'Donald! You're not supposed to bite the dog!' and my brother just said 'Well, he bit me first.' That's just how he was back then and he still is today. Donald's a wonderful person; just don't bite him."

Donald loved animals. One Easter, his father brought home a baby chick for a pet. Everyone knew that someday, when the chick was grown, it would end up as Sunday dinner. "When the day finally came," says Rena, "Donald wouldn't touch the food. In fact, he wouldn't eat chicken again for a long, long time."

The following year, Rivers brought home a baby rabbit as an Easter gift for the children. Donald was enchanted by the soft, silky bunny, and loved to bring it bits of food. But the rabbit's bottomless cage sat directly on the ground and when the rabbit finally dug its way to freedom, Donald cried bitterly with disappointment.

"He probably wouldn't want people to know that," admits Rena. "Anyway, after that, our father said he was never going to bring another animal home again, and I don't think he ever did."

At age nine, Donald, who rarely ever got sick, managed to come down with pneumonia. The infection felt like a trash barrel sitting on his chest and the fever and weakness overwhelmed him as he lay exhausted in his bed, waiting and waiting to get better. When no improvement came, Donald's mother sent for the doctor to come by the house and see what he could do.

Although he wasn't especially tall, the doctor looked somehow bigger than Donald's father, and although surely not as strong, he seemed infinitely more powerful. Donald immediately sat up on the edge of his bed. Through the opening of the doctor's intriguing leather bag, Donald could just see the tops of small glass jars, shiny metal instruments, small wooden-handled tools of some kind, and all sorts of other fascinating, unidentifiable objects.

The doctor thrust his experienced hand deep inside the bag and drew out a small dark bottle of liquid and a clear glass syringe, to which he quickly attached a silvery needle. Exactly how the liquid got inside the syringe, Donald wasn't quite sure. But within seconds the doctor was at Donald's bedside, plunging the thick needle deep into the firm flesh of Donald's left butt.

> *It hurt like hell, but the next morning, I felt fine. The fever was gone and I wasn't sick any more. Knowing what I know now about medicine, the doctor could have easily given me the wrong stuff. He maybe even could have killed me. But at the time, it seemed like magic: I was sick, he gave me a shot, and I was better.*
>
> *I just decided that's what I wanted to do someday. I wanted to be a doctor.*

Right then and there, at nine years old, Donald decided on his life's work: to be a doctor, to help the sick, to solve problems no one else— not even his own powerful father—could solve. To be the one giving the shots.

Never mind that it was 1945. Never mind that Martin Luther King, Jr., was himself still a child. At the tender age of nine, Donald Edward Wilson—this little boy, this little black kid living in mostly white Worcester, Massachusetts, back before the Civil Rights Movement of the 1960s, back before *Brown vs. the Board of Education* in 1954, back in the days when colored folks rarely even went inside a medical school except maybe to sweep up, this brilliant child who got straight A's without trying, who hauled trash with his father for six grueling hours a day in the hot summer months, this small brown boy in a big white world— "just decided" to become a doctor.

Of course, to hear him talk about it as an adult, you might think he merely decided to wear one shirt instead or another.

> *Really, it was no big deal. I was sick, the doctor came in, he gave me a shot, and I got better. So I decided to be a doctor. That's all.*

And to him, it really was "no big deal." But it was a real commitment.

> *My sister and mother thought it was just a lark, but it never left my mind.*

Few things do.

With a memory like a steel vault, Donald found school to be quite effortless. He did so well, that he eventually had to be moved into a class for gifted children in the 7th and 8th grades. And even among these high-achievers, Donald rose above the crowd.

Meanwhile, like pennies collecting in a cookie jar, Rivers gave Donald more and more responsibilities.

> *My father always treated me like an adult from as early as I can remember. When I was barely a teenager, he would send me around to collect money from his various tenants. Can you imagine sending a twelve-year-old around these days with hundreds of dollars in their pocket? My father showed me a lot of faith.*

But despite Donald's hard work at home and stellar achievements at school, when it came time for the rest of his class to advance to high school, Donald's principal was sincerely concerned. What was the point, he wondered, of a black boy going on to North High School where the white college-bound students go? Wouldn't it make a lot more sense for Donald to go to the vocational Boy's Trade School, where he could "learn a trade and get a decent job?"

Donald's parents went down to the school and told the principle their son was more than qualified to go to college-preparatory North High School and that was exactly where he was going. "Besides," thought Donald. "I don't want just 'a decent job,' I want to be a doctor."

At North High School, Donald continued to find his school work to be effortless. North High was truly a diverse institution: a lot of Italians, Irish, Armenians, Greeks, and two black students. But Donald fit right in. He considers many of his classmates to be true friends and recalls few acts of racism. Even today, he attends his high school class reunions and is warmly welcomed, as well as revered.

Even with making high grades in all his subjects, Donald still had plenty of time to run on the school's cross-country track team, compete on the basketball team, volunteer at the school's library as the head of the Student Library Committee, and serve as Editor-in-Chief of the high school Year Book—all while maintaining a top spot on the school's honor roll every semester and being named a Horace Mann Student, a title reserved only for the tiniest handful of students who earned all A's for at least two consecutive years.

In his senior year, his peers aptly voted him "Most likely to succeed," and under his Year Book picture they added the words: "His achievements speak for themselves."

But even straight A's and plenty of extra-curricular activities weren't enough to fully occupy Donald Wilson. So in his "spare" time, when he wasn't going to school, playing a sport, attending church, volunteering at the library, hauling trash, or collecting the rent on his father's properties, Donald tried his hand at a variety of odd jobs.

When I was maybe thirteen, I went door-to-door, trying to sell fountain pens. You know how it goes: People in your immediate family would buy that worthless junk so you could make a few bucks. It wasn't for me. I'd never succeed as a sales person; I hate asking people to buy things.

When I was fourteen and old enough for a real job, I worked at the local bowling alley as a pin boy. That was back before they had the automatic pin setters so the bowling pins had to be quickly reset each time by hand. In Massachusetts, instead of using the big "10 pins," we had smaller candle pins. For six months, I'd go down to the bowling alley and set and reset pins. It was pretty strenuous work. You have to spot the pins accurately and keep up with the bowlers. The trick was to get in there right after the third ball hit the pins and get the balls back and all the pins back up within ten seconds. I didn't like that job.

Then in high school, I worked for a year or so as an office boy at our local newspaper, <u>The Worcester Telegram and Gazette</u>. I worked two nights a week from five to eleven o'clock, and all day Sunday. Mostly, I filed papers and I clipped articles from the newspaper that required some kind of follow-up. On the weekends, I watched the switchboard operator, and eventually I learned how to use the switchboard. People would always call the newspaper, looking for information, and I would go look it up. It beat setting up pins.

Of course, every summer until I was maybe nineteen or twenty, I hauled trash with my father. He'd come and wake me up early every morning, except Sunday, and we'd go until about two o'clock. He always paid me, unless we were doing some work on one of his rental properties. Then heed say, "That's going to be your property someday, so I'm not going to pay you for that."

21

Even with work and school, Donald found time for friends on both sides of the tracks.

> *I always had black friends and white friends. My mother didn't mind me dating a few white girls, but she'd always warn: "Don't get too serious." As I got older, my interests just naturally led me to the black girls and boys on the East Side.*
>
> *Being a teenager in Worcester was relatively uncomplicated then. I had a small group of friends, boys and girls, and we got together every weekend at someone's house to listen to music, take in a movie, or just hang around. Even when the inevitable "pairing off" began to occur, we remained a close group.*
>
> *I knew that racism was there, but we mostly avoided it by keeping to ourselves. Once, three of my friends and I went to a restaurant that featured fried clam and scallop dinners (a New England favorite), all you could eat for $1.49. One of my friends could eat a lot. When he ordered his fourth plate the manager refused saying he was sharing his food with us (which he wasn't) and therefore the all-you-could-eat clause was voided. We refused to leave, insisting that he was entitled to his meal. Even if he was sharing food with us we had all paid for the all-you-could-eat promotion.*
>
> *The manager called the police and two big Irish cops arrived, refused to listen to anything we had to say and told us to leave or go to jail. I doubt that would have happened if we were white.*
>
> *I've lost track of most of the people I knew in Worcester, but believe it or not, even after a half a century, I still talk to my first girlfriend every once in a while. We're still friends.*

Even back then, talking was one of Donald's specialties. Not that he was overly chatty or even especially outgoing. But his command, not only of the language, but of the persuasive power of logic, made him hard to ignore and even harder to win an argument against.

> *My classmates and teachers used to tell me I should be a lawyer because there was rarely an argument I couldn't win. One time, during a class debate, they really thought they had me. The debate question was: If a man spends ten years of his life sweeping floors for a living, has he made any progress in his career? The seemingly logical answer, of course, was No. How could anyone who swept floors for a decade be said to have made any progress? But my assignment was to argue that Yes, he had progressed.*
>
> *First, my opponent made all the predictable points about how the poor guy hadn't gotten anywhere in ten years. Then it was my turn and I'm sure everyone thought I was done for—until I started describing, in detail, how this hard-working veteran floor sweeper, over the course of about five hundred weeks of labor, had naturally learned a tremendous amount about exactly which floor-sweeping techniques made his job more effective and efficient, and what brooms did the best job, and how best to hold the broom, and how to clean each kind of floor, depending on the materials in question. After ten years of on-the-job experience, of course the man progressed in his career!*

And, of course, Donald won the debate. But being a lawyer wasn't what he was after. As an eighteen-year-old, now twice the age he was when the man with the magic bag miraculously made him well, Donald still had his mind set on going to medical school. All he needed to do was take care of one small detail: college.

So, in 1954, during his senior year, he applied to two nearby schools:

> *Clark University, because they were lusting after me because of my grades and class standing, and Bates College, because I didn't know any better. A couple of kids at my high school were talking about how great Bates was, so I thought I wanted to go there. Both schools were salivating over me. They even offered me money I never asked for.*

Then the High School assistant principal, a Harvard alumnus, had an intriguing idea. "Why don't you apply to my school?"

> *It just hadn't occurred to me before. So I applied to Harvard the day before the deadline. My parents didn't know about it at the time. When I told them later, they just said OK. It was no big deal.*

But it was a big deal. No one in Donald's family had ever gone to college before. In fact, few blacks in Worcester or any U.S. town went to college prior to 1954, which was also the year that *Brown vs. the Board of Education of Topeka Kansas* banned segregation in all public schools.

Surely, his impeccable grades and class standing would easily get him into Clark or Bates. But when Harvard never called him for an interview, well, Donald just figured he didn't make the cut.

Then came the letter.

At first, he thought it might be one of those rejection notes, perhaps something along the lines of "While we found your application to be quite impressive, we regret to inform you..." Blah, blah, blah.

But then, again, you never know until you open it. After all, another kid in his class, a kid who *did* get called in for an interview, had just gotten the very same size letter from Harvard on the very same day—and *he* got in...

Nah. No interview. No interview, no getting in.

Then he ripped open the envelope and there it was, in black ink on heavy cream-colored stationary: "Harvard University is pleased to inform you…"

Donald Wilson was not a young man given to outburst of emotion, but this one would be hard to contain. In a private moment, the blood rushed quietly to his face.

Harvard University. Even the name sounded important! Of course he would go. Of course he would do well.

But how well? Just how well would this big fish, who had grown so agile and strong in his relatively small pond, be able to swim among the blue-bloods, the silver-spoons, the geniuses, and the otherwise endowed?

How well? As well as he pleased.

The next day, Donald sent Harvard a letter confirming he would attend. Soon, thick packets of papers, radiating with the crimson Harvard emblem, began arriving in the Wilson's mailbox: housing applications, medical history forms, instructions for freshman, class schedules, maps, and of course, financial aid forms.

Tuition was $600 a year. Room and board cost another $2,000. With books and other expenses, it would come to about $3,000, a considerable sum in 1954. Donald poured over all the materials and eagerly completed each form.

But the more questions he had to ask his father about family finances as he filled out the detailed financial aid application, the more agitated his father became.

"All this stuff about how much I make, how much I save, how much I have and where I keep it—all this stuff is nobody's business," said Rivers, who hated the idea of letting any person or institution know too much about his personal business.

"I take care of my money and I take care of my family, and I'm not about to tell Harvard University or anybody else about my affairs."

A moment or two later, it was all settled. Forget the questions. Forget the financial aid forms. In fact, forget the financial aid all together. Donald's father would *pay in full* for Donald to attend college—for his fancy Ivy League tuition, his fancy books, his room and board, his laboratory expenses—all of it.

Rivers Wilson, the trash-hauler, the home-owner, the self-made real estate tycoon, the boy who ran for his life to avoid being lynched because he looked a white man in the eye, would gather up all those pennies he had steadily grown into dollars, and pay in cash for his only son Donald Edward Wilson *to go to college.*

To go to *Harvard University.*

Horace Mann Honor Students. North High School, Worcester, MA. 1954

Pennies From Heaven

High School Basketball 1953

CHAPTER 3

Becoming Doctor Wilson
Smart, Black, and On Track

"We're gonna rock around the clock tonight"
"Rock Around the Clock"
By Max C. Friedman and James
E. Myers

Daring to take on four years of college, plus four more years of medical school, followed by a hundred-twenty hour per week year-long medical internship, and then three years of medical residencies, Donald Wilson rolled into Cambridge, Massachusetts, in September 1954 as eager as Bill Haley and His Comets to "Rock Around the Clock."

Of course, when the quick-witted, trash-hauling son of Rivers and Licine Wilson first arrived on the pristine campus of Harvard University that fall, with his bags neatly packed and his mind primed for action, few people outside his immediate family thought he'd get very far.

While most of the country was settling comfortably into what could have been called the Decade of the Den, the relaxed 1950s were not equally welcoming to all. For the majority of white Americans, the 1950s—lounging safely between World War II of the 1940s and the social upheaval of the 1960s—was a time of bobby socks, poodle skirts, cookie-cutter suburbs, and the instantly popular Swanson "TV Dinner," a single serving of roast turkey, stuffing, potatoes, and peas frozen into an aluminum tray that could be individually reheated, carried to the couch, and eaten in front of the tube.

But for most minority Americans, the 1950s were neither comfortable nor especially convenient, particularly if you happened to be an ambitious, intellectually gifted, young black man with his heart set on becoming a physician. Big important careers, or for that matter, *any* career requiring a college education, were about as easy for an African American to achieve in 1954 as scaling Mt. Everest in a whiteout.

The numbers weren't good.

In fact, when eighteen-year-old Donald finished hauling trash with his father through the long hot summer and eagerly began packing for school that fall, less than one in about fifteen hundred students attending majority U.S. colleges were African-American. And with nearly no minority professors on campus and so few minority professionals off campus, African-American students often discovered that making it into college was no guarantee of making it *through* college. The truth was that most majority U.S. colleges in the mid 1950s graduated no minority students at all.

Harvard University's numbers were well ahead of the national average, but that wasn't saying too much. In 1954, only nine of Harvard's 1,162 undergraduate freshmen were African-American. Established in 1636, America's oldest institution of higher learning admitted its first negro student way back in 1865. But the campus remained so racially segregated over the years that its few minority students may well have agreed with Booker T. Washington, who upon receiving an honorary masters degree from Harvard in 1896 said "I feel like a huckleberry in a bowl of milk."

For more than three centuries, Harvard graduated many powerful and influential Americans. Among them were six presidents, more than three dozen Nobel laureates, and thousands of successful scientists, politicians, academics, entrepreneurs, and others in pursuit of the American Dream with names like Rockefeller, Stevenson, and Kahn.

So when a little fish from nearby Worcester dove head first into Harvard's vast white ocean of history, achievement, and prestige, few people on campus expected much more from Wilson than to keep his head above water.

After all, *he got in*. Wasn't that enough?

Merely staying afloat, however, was the last thing on Donald's mind. Forget the numbers. Forget the racist assumptions. Forget the fact that just last year someone had burned a cross right there in the middle of Harvard Yard. He had come to Harvard to learn what he could, get into medical school, and become a doctor. That was The Plan. And as always, Donald Wilson fully expected to succeed.

Freshman Orientation

Ready to get rolling, Donald and more than a thousand other new students sat in Memorial Hall on a warm September day in 1954, waiting for Freshman Orientation to officially begin. In reality, Donald's Harvard "orientation" was already well underway. Portraits of former University presidents, deans, and benefactors stared down from their walls in what seemed like a suffocating mixture of enlightenment, pride, and disdain. Donald glanced around the huge hall as the other students talked quietly to their neighbors, stared nervously off into space, or leafed anxiously through their new Harvard University folders.

Surveying the room, Donald couldn't help but notice how quickly many students turned away when his brown face momentarily met theirs. As in high school, few students in the room looked like him. But unlike at his previous school, here a bit of a chill pervaded the air—not open hostility, no name-calling, no crowd of white hoods carrying a tangle of rope, just a bit of a chill. It was a cool academic climate Donald would learn to live with for many years.

> *I remember being impressed by Harvard, by its sheer size and the brilliance of the people there—not overwhelmed, but impressed. You've got to remember this was before the days of affirmative action and, in a class of 1,162 people, just nine of us were African-American. There was no interest on the part of Harvard to diversify. Back then, Harvard's idea of "diversity" was how many other countries their students came from, not what color they were. As it turned out, one of the black students wasn't even African-American; he was African. So really, there were only eight of us.*

Soon after the first-day speeches ended, Donald and the rest of the newcomers were directed to pick up their student housing packets from the long, linen-draped tables in the back of the hall. Opening the heavy, cream-colored envelop, Donald soon discovered he would not be living with the rest of the freshman in Harvard Yard. Instead, he would be placed a short distance away on Holyoke Street with a handful of other students.

> *They said they didn't have enough room for us. Maybe we were misfits or something.*

Back in his father's day in South Carolina, such things were far less mysterious. In the Deep South, most whites were about as willing to share a room with a black man as they were to sleep with a snake. But in Massachusetts in the mid-1950s, such racism was somewhat more subdued. Not gone, mind you, just more refined.

Within hours of being placed outside Harvard Yard, Donald discovered that his originally assigned roommate had mysteriously disappeared, replaced by two others who were more willing, or at least less unwilling, to share living quarters with him.

> *I don't know who my original roommate was, but he opted out as soon as he "found out." He just said No Thanks. So everything was quickly reshuffled and I was placed with two guys with Jewish-sounding names. The interesting thing was that, all of a sudden, I was in a room with ostensibly two Jews—except it turned out one of them wasn't even Jewish. He was German, which was hilarious. We became fast friends.*

Donald and German roommate Richard Rohrberg spent many hours together studying, playing sports, and checking out the local jazz clubs. When they had the time, the roommates socialized with a handful of both white and black students at the local beer pub. Occasionally, Donald would toss a few basketballs with whomever was willing to play.

> *I was aware of the wealth. Adlai Stevenson III was on campus at that time, as was Jay Rockefeller. I played basketball with Jay a few times.*

Blazing His Trail

Despite his small group of friends, Donald was essentially on his own. As often was the case for minority students who managed to get into majority colleges in the 1950s, Donald had not a single teacher, role model, or mentor to take him under their wing or to point the way. Effectively advisor-less for his entire education, Donald was left on his own with countless educational decisions, big and small: what courses to take, what electives to try, which teachers to avoid, how and when to pick a major.

Being accustomed to hard work, Donald instinctively selected a heavy load of all science classes for the biology major, on track for medical school. The work was challenging, but not intimidating. Donald attended every class, plowed through the homework, and scored well on every test. By the end of his freshman year, to the surprise of some people at the school, Donald made the Dean's list.

> *In my freshman year, my entire visit with my so-called advisor amounted to "Oh, you know, you've done much better here than we expected you to do. We expected you to be in the bottom quarter of the class, but you are in the top quarter of the class. That's unexpected. Very nice to see you. Good-bye."*
>
> *I never went back. There obviously wasn't much he could advise me about.*

Although his grades were good, Donald found it increasingly difficult to remain immune to the school's low expectations of him. With no one pushing him to excel and with few opportunities for most freshman to standout, Donald's motivation began to wane. Back in high school, everyday was a new opportunity to come to class on the top of his game, prove what he knew, and soak up even more. At Harvard, freshman simply sat passively, day after day, silently taking notes. Other than on tests and term papers, there were few real challenges, no formal debates, not many ways for Donald to shine.

> *Harvard was much less personal, and in many respects, a lot less formal than what I was used to. The classes were large and you weren't often called upon to give answers. You were just one in a mass of people. I found there was less motivation for me to study and excel. I made the Dean's List, but I clearly was no longer at the top of my class. Maybe no matter what I did I wouldn't have been at the top of my class. But part of the motivation for excelling for me was people looking at me and saying, "Gee, that guy really knows his stuff," and since that wasn't available for me at Harvard, that pushing factor no longer existed.*

> *So instead of being an all-A student, I became a mixed student. I did well, but I was not at the top of my class. Of course, being anywhere in your class at Harvard usually gives you a leg up on most anybody else in the country. At least it did back then.*

In addition to attending lectures, taking lab classes, tackling homework, writing term papers, and studying for exams, Donald spent his "spare time" shelving books in the school library. It was tedious work, but not anything compared to hauling trash. Besides, he could use the extra cash to occasionally join his friends for a beer or two, or to go to a Harvard football game, especially if they were playing Yale.

For the next two years, Donald and Richard lived in Lowell House, an undergraduate residence hall where the two friends often stayed up late into the night talking, working on assignments, or studying for exams. Every weekend, despite his workload, Donald would faithfully drive the forty or so miles back to his parents' home to wash his clothes, get a decent home-cooked meal, and relax in the rare company of folks who knew in their bones he would succeed.

Plus, back in Worcester was Donald's girlfriend, Valerie who he married after graduation.

> *Most of the few African-American girls at Radcliff tried to pretend they were white. I didn't like that, but I understood it. If you are constantly told you are no good, that you are inferior, and then you start succeeding and hanging out with white people, you may begin to only associate with white people, and eventually you may try to be white yourself. This happened with college girls, especially. I understood it, but I never dated any of them.*

Double-dating with other Harvard students, or on their own, Bill Bronson and Donald enjoyed going to Jazz clubs in Boston, where they would nurse a couple of beers and listen to musicians like Charlie Parker, Stan Getz, and Dave Brubeck.

During summer breaks, Donald returned to Worcester to work full time, no longer hauling trash with his father, but hauling mental patients around in the local State Hospital. As an orderly there, he quickly discovered that handling tons of trash under the hot summer sun was far easier—and more lucrative—than dealing with mentally ill patients. Still, he stuck with the grueling hospital work every summer until graduation. This was his first professional experience in medicine, and Donald grabbed it with both hands.

> *Back in those days, mentally ill people were really disturbed, and violently so. Hospitals were just beginning to use medications like Serpasil and Thorazine to quiet people down. They gave them enough to make them zombies and they locked them in wards. There were a lot of people locked up, and the most violent ones were locked into single rooms. With some, you were told you had to approach them in a very special way or they might kill you. I assisted with a lot of Electric Shock Therapy. This was before they used muscle relaxants. My function with the patient was primarily to help control the convulsions. I was there to help hold them down. Actually, we were holding their shoulder joints in place so that they wouldn't dislocate them. It wasn't a very pretty sight.*

No matter what happened at State Hospital each summer, Donald returned to Harvard every fall as determined as ever to be a physician. And when the time came to apply to medical schools in his senior year,

Donald Wilson did what Donald Wilson always does: He did it his way. With no mentors anywhere in sight, that's just the way it was.

Tufts University and Boston University looked good, and they were close to home. He also applied to Howard University Medical School in Washington, D.C., "because it seemed like a good idea." But, oddly, considering his ambitions, Donald never applied to Harvard. He said it just never occurred to him, although it probably would have occurred to an interested advisor, had there been one. Years later, with the wisdom of time, it became easier to understand this omission.

> *A lot of the people who went to Tufts did so because they didn't get into Harvard Medical School. I never applied to Harvard, possibly because I didn't think I would get in and I didn't want to get rejected.*
>
> *In retrospect, I probably should have applied to Harvard. But the truth is I didn't like Harvard that much. It was too big. It was too snooty. And the six of us who were graduating African-Americans were looked at as curiosities. I hadn't heard anything better about the medical school. I talked to a few African-Americans who had graduated from Harvard Medical School and they had a miserable time when they were there. It didn't strike me that things were going to get any better.*

Given his high academic standing, it was no surprise that all three schools wanted him. Not keen on leaving the area, Donald quickly narrowed his choices to Tufts and Boston University.

> *Tufts had a better reputation, but at first I was going to go to BU because actually BU had nicer buildings and was a little bit smaller. Tufts was located in a modified warehouse in downtown Boston. It had nothing to recommend it other than its reputation. So I was going to go to BU until I visited the school and*

discovered that at BU they posted your grades after every test. You would have a test and then the next day everybody's grade would be up on a bulletin board. Having spent four years at Harvard, I wasn't used to that kind of Mickey Mouse stuff, which I felt was counter-productive. That didn't make any sense to me and it seemed unnecessarily competitive. Why should you know what my grade was on yesterday's test? That's too much dog-eat-dog. Tufts didn't do anything like that so I decided to go to Tufts. And that's the only reason I ended up there.

So the decision was made. He would spend the next four years at Tufts University Medical School in Boston, not far from his family, and well on the road to becoming Doctor Wilson.

Everything seemed to be rolling along as planned, until in the last semester of his last year at Harvard, Donald decided to "try something different." The elective history course should have been a cake-walk after all those rigorous science classes, but instead of getting an easy A, the unthinkable happened.

The class was History of the South, taught by a white southerner, and he and I were constantly at odds over his concept of the history of the South and my concept of the history of the South. He thought it was all just glorious, just a wonderful experience. He didn't see where there was much depression and what was wrong with all these happy, friendly "darkies." According to his version of history, everything was just dandy until a bunch of northerners came along and got them all riled up, making them think they wanted to vote.

You have to remember, this was 1958, before the civil rights movement of the 1960s. Everybody just went along with what this guy was trying to tell us. Everyone, except me.

> *In those days, these kinds of courses were all essay. There was never any objective exam. You would write an essay about your thoughts on a topic and the professor would sit down and see how he liked your essay. I wrote what I knew about the real history of the South, and it had little to do with the nonsense he was trying to teach us. He didn't have the guts to fail me, so he did the next best thing.*

He opened his final grades report and there it was. For the first time in his life Donald Edward Wilson had gotten a D. For a thin sliver of time, a silent shock wave pulsed through his core. But within seconds, Donald knew it mattered not at all. Here he stood, on the threshold of his life in the spring of 1958: the first person in his family to go to college, the son of a hardworking entrepreneur who escaped being lynched and paid cash for his son to attend Harvard University, one of six African-American graduates who would walk tall in a sea of thousands, a strong young man with his mind made up, his feet on the ground, his new bride by his side, and an acceptance letter to one of nation's top medical school in his pocket, and no plantation-revisionist history instructor could do a damn thing about it.

Donald's entire family was elated about the coming commencement. His sister Rena bought a new pair of shoes for the occasion. Rivers Wilson would wear his best suit. But tragically, Donald's mother never got to see her son become the physician her little boy had dreamed he would someday be. In May, 1958, just weeks before Donald graduated from Harvard University, Licine Wilson died.

No one knew exactly why it happened, but Donald knew enough to know it probably shouldn't have.

> *She was in the hospital with pneumonia for about three or four days, got well, came home. And the day she came home she died. I don't know exactly what happened. My guess is she probably*

> *had a pulmonary embolism. I'll never know for sure. What I do know is that the doctor who was taking care of her didn't know very much. It was all a big show, probably not unlike a lot of practicing doctors who had not really kept up and didn't really know what was going on. The reason they were successful most of the time was because most people get better no matter what you do to them.*

Whatever he did with his life, Donald knew he wasn't going to be *that* kind of doctor.

Toughing It Out at Tufts

A Harvard diploma could open many doors in Boston, but for people of color in 1958, an apartment in Cambridge where Donald and his wife had hoped to live while he attended Tufts Medical School was definitely not one of them.

> *The landlords just came right out and said, "We don't rent to coloreds." One even asked me where I had been living and I said right here in Cambridge, but then I remembered I had been living on university property.*

Unable to find anyone else to take their rent, the couple settled in a tiny place on Seaver Street in Dorchester, as Donald readied himself to climb his next mountain.

Back in those days, the first year of medical school was less about training future physicians than it was a brutal initiation, almost a hazing, as new medical students struggled to survive their first year of trial-by-fire boot camp.

> *Those were the days when they tried to make things as miserable as possible for you. The idea was to see if they could make you*

so miserable that you'd leave. Their idea was that if you were one of those who stayed you were destined to be a good doctor. If you couldn't get through all their hurtles and roadblocks, you shouldn't be there anyway.

On my first day of medical school, the teacher who spoke at Freshman Orientation said, "Look to your left; look to your right. One of you three people will not be here at graduation." It really was a sink-or-swim mentality.

Medical students today really have no idea of what it used to be like. The medical education process was really pretty bad. It was a very traumatic experience. Over the years, it has become much more humane. The approach now is everybody who enters will graduate unless they later decide they don't want to become a physician or something unexpected happens.

With his mother recently gone, his new wife ill, and the couple struggling to survive on about five dollars a week, Donald found medical school to be far more difficult, far more frustrating, and far more boring than he ever imagined. It was so bad that just weeks into his first semester at Tufts, Donald began to wonder if he would bother to stay.

I didn't like medical school. Immediately, within weeks, I just didn't like it. I thought the first year of medical school was disgusting. I didn't see the relevance of some of the things they made you do. I didn't like the dissection of the cadavers, picking through all these tissues and so forth, or spending time with a microscope and slides and tissues. I don't remember anybody being helpful in the first year.

For example, in biochemistry, our professor was the chairman of the department of biochemistry. In his first introduction to us he said he didn't particularly like medical students. He said he didn't think medical students were very bright. They

> *weren't interested in biochemistry, and the only reason he was there was to do his research. He tolerated it but he really didn't like teaching us. I thought that was pretty ballsy for a guy who was at a medical school to have the colossal gall to tell medical students he didn't care about them. The fact that a medical school would allow a chairman to say that to students, and get away with it, made it clear what kind of place it was.*

Like Harvard, Tufts University had no interest in diversity. Of 114 first-year medical students at Tufts that September, only Donald and two others were African-American. Retention would not be an issue. Two had come from Harvard, the third from Wellesley. Across the country, minorities represented only about 2 percent of medical school students in 1958. And most of those students were attending either Howard or Meharry. Non-minority schools like Tufts had very few students and some had none.

As was the case at Harvard, Tufts had no African-American faculty or other professionals to serve as role models or mentors. In fact, at no time in his entire four years of medical school, nor even during his year-long internship, did Donald see a single African-American physician. *Not even one.* There were times it seemed that no one who looked like him had ever passed this way before. But Donald had little time to dwell on such thoughts. In the intense pressure-cooker environment of first-year medical school, nearly every student had but a single focus: Getting through it.

> *As I remember it, we were all being harassed equally. In medical school in 1958, you were so stressed out you didn't have time to think about things like race. All you could think about was surviving. In that kind of a situation, you develop some kind of camaraderie.*

Donald and his classmates scrambled to keep up with an impossible workload, punctuated by what often seemed to be meaningless laboratory exercises and hours of pointless cadaver dissections. There were times it all just seemed so pointless. With no mentor to help him over the hump, he could have easily slipped through the cracks of his own dissatisfaction and quit right then and there.

Fortunately, a brief conversation with a first-year teacher provided just enough minimal support to keep him going a bit longer.

> *I told one of the professors—this guy teaching histology, his name was MaGruder—that I was quitting at the end of the first semester. I said, "I think after Christmas, I won't bother coming back." He talked me into staying through the first year. "You can always quit," he said. "Why don't you wait until the end of the year and if you still want to quit, then quit, but don't quit in the middle of the year."*

Despite feeling terribly unhappy, Donald's rational mind, as always, was firmly in charge. The professor's advice sounded rational, so he stayed.

The following year, things started looking up.

> *In the second year, they let you get more involved with patients, so you saw some relevance in what you were doing and why you went to medical school. You also got to deal with more interesting teachers. The first year of medical school really had nothing to do with becoming a doctor. It was like another year of undergraduate work. The second year you had the opportunity to interact with patients and it got to be fun. Things began to make more sense to me. I was glad I stayed.*

Practical applications, logical connections, hands-on experience, and an opportunity to put knowledge to work in the real world all appealed to Donald far more than picking through dead bodies.

> *The second year is when you started physical diagnosis. You'd go with an instructor on Rounds and you'd talk to patients, examining them. The instructor would go over it with you and see if you had gotten the history right or if you picked up the physical findings and this and that and the other thing. And the good thing was that they used people who were not employed faculty at the medical school. They had faculty appointments but they were volunteer faculty. So you would go off to different hospitals where that faculty member might happen to be practicing and he would cover his own patients, for example. It was fun because the guys who usually did this did it because they enjoyed doing it. They weren't getting any money out of it but they enjoyed having medical students around.*

Although he only got a taste of "real medicine" about once a week, the experience energized him enough to get through his classes and complete his labs. Soon, his grades improved, his determination returned, and Donald was back on track and running at full hilt toward his goal.

Committing fully to his work again felt good, but the demands of medical school left little time or energy for the rest of his life. Donald only occasionally socialized with fellow classmates and saw less of his new bride than either would have liked.

> *Some of us would get together from time to time. The most expensive thing we could have was beer. Nobody could afford anything other than beer. We'd do that occasionally together. A significant part of the class was married. It was just beginning to change where medical students were getting married.*

> *The powers that be felt it was a big interference with medical school and they really didn't want you to do it. At the time, I didn't understand, but now I can see they were right. It was a big interference.*

As usual, Donald dealt with the pressures, both on and off campus, on his own and with little support. Despite a loving family, a new wife, and handful of good friends, when it came to his career, Donald was essentially on his own. For better or worse, he would make his own way. Most of the time, Donald considered the absence of role models or mentors as no more than an inconvenience, an added burden when calculating his next logical best step.

But occasionally, a thought gnawed at the back of his mind, *what if...*

> *I suspect that other students did have that type of relationship. I didn't. I didn't find anybody who I felt was particularly interested in me. Sometimes, I wonder what might have happened differently if I did.*

Nonetheless, Donald persisted and prevailed. And after a while he discovered that when he donned his white coat and carried his black bag out into the world, plenty of people were interested, even grateful to see him.

> *The nice thing about medical school—the enjoyable part—is when we used to go on house calls to different communities as part of community medicine projects. Obviously, we'd see poor people who couldn't afford to have a physician. I got assigned to a place called Columbia Point, which was a little community almost totally separated from the rest of Boston, jutting out into the harbor. I believe there were mostly white people there. It*

> was a rough area. But the interesting thing is the families were so grateful for anything that you could do. I wouldn't go to South Boston because South Boston was so racist I probably couldn't have gotten out of there alive. East Boston wasn't much better. But in Columbia Point, I don't ever recall going in a home where a mother didn't offer me a cookie or a cup of coffee or something like that. Normally, I would never have gone there, but as long as I was walking around with my black bag, I knew nobody would ever touch me. They knew I was there providing a service that nobody could afford and they would leave me alone. They were very grateful. I was touched by that.

The experience of actually *doing* medicine—of thinking through the diagnosis and taking care of patients—made Donald feel energized, necessary, and important. By the time he graduated from Tufts in 1962, Donald was chomping at the bit to conquer his next two hurtles: the internship and residency.

> Back then you had to do a year's internship, and then generally speaking, you did three years of residency following that. I did a rotating internship at St. Elizabeth's Hospital in Boston. In a rotating internship, you spent time in medicine, pediatrics, surgery, obstetrics/gynecology, and a few other specialties.
> At first, I thought that I might want to do pediatrics, but after a couple of months on pediatrics, I decided it would be medicine. I didn't like dealing with the mothers. So I decided to go into internal medicine, and it's interesting how fate would have it. At St. Elizabeth's they did not invite me to stay on as a resident in internal medicine because I was too independent. I've always been reasonably outspoken and I don't tolerate oppression very well.

The oppression, in this case, wasn't about race but the abusive working conditions imposed on the lowest man on the hospital totem pole: the mere medical intern.

Not on My Shift

Medical interns today often complain about having to endure a sixty-hour workweek. Back in 1962, such limited hours would have been considered part-time. Interns at St. Elizabeth's Hospital and other hospitals routinely worked a good solid *hundred-twenty hours* a week. We worked all day, every other night, and every other weekend—with little or no sleep.

Donald recalls it as "the most miserable existence you can imagine." But that's just how it was back then, and the sadistic tradition often baffled and frustrated Donald. Sacrifice and hard work were one thing, but illogical inefficiencies were always hard for Donald Wilson to accept. A more rational schedule would not only have benefited the battered interns, it would have boosted overall productivity and improved patient care.

For several months on this ridiculous schedule, Donald showed up, did his job, and kept his mouth shut. But intelligent, independent thinkers who care deeply about their work don't tolerate irrational conditions very well, or for very long.

Finally, on the third weekend in January 1963, Donald drew a line in the sand. He had come in at seven on Saturday morning and would not be allowed to leave until about six Monday evening. Around two o'clock Saturday afternoon, Donald got his first admission. The man wasn't in need of immediate medial care, but back in those days doctors sent their patients in to the hospital for medical tests and "workups." By three o'clock, four more people were admitted. By six o'clock another five showed up. By nine o'clock that night, Donald had twenty-five admissions!

> *Now there is no way anybody can adequately work up twenty-five new patients in less than fifteen hours, while at the same time answering emergency calls from nurses and other patients. So it was simply mathematically impossible to effectively see all these people in the time I had. These days, our interns rarely receive twenty-five new patients in a week.*
>
> *And you know why I had all these new patients? Not because they were sick, but because the internists were trying to get their patients into hospital beds on Saturday before the surgeons tried to get their patients, who were scheduled for surgery on Monday morning, into the beds on Sunday. The whole thing was just a big turf fight for beds. Most of these people weren't even sick. They were just coming in for work-ups.*

Donald called the hospital's senior medical resident and told him flat out that the situation was intolerable. He had a flood of twenty-five admissions and he clearly needed help.

"Oh, yeah," replied the resident, flatly. "That's too bad. That's really terrible."

Donald asked him what exactly he planned to do about it. Was he going to come down and work up some of these admissions with him or what?

"Oh, no," laughed the resident. "I had to go through all that when I was an intern. Now it's your turn. You are just going to have to do it all yourself."

For a brief moment, Donald rationally contemplated the futility of the situation. He logically pondered the reality he was facing, calculated the time available, and weighed the needs of his sick patients who would be forced to wait while he admitted so many others who were not especially ill. Then, without hesitation, he let the senior resident have it with both barrels.

Becoming Doctor Wilson

"I'll tell you what," Donald explained, getting right to the point. "You've got two choices: Either you come down here and you work up some of these patients with me, or you come down here and work them all up by yourself, because I will be going home."

The senior resident hadn't worked up a patient in years. That night he did.

Later that same weekend, Donald challenged other "irrational conditions" at the hospital. It wasn't a matter of rebelling against too much work. No logical work challenge was too much for the young doctor--*if that challenge made sense*. But plain old stupidity was simply not acceptable to Donald Wilson, not as an intern at St. Elizabeth's and not anywhere ever since. While many would later find this trait to be a mark of a true leader, not everyone was especially pleased.

Donald's last admission came in around eleven o'clock that night in the private sector of the hospital. He had expected to find someone suffering from pneumonia, but when he got to the room he discovered a well-dressed seventeen-year-old girl sitting on the edge of the bed watching television and smoking a Benson & Hedges cigarette.

Donald bristled at the sight of the apparently healthy girl with the fancy smoke dangling from her nearly manicured hand.

"What's wrong with you?" he asked.

"Nothing," she said.

"Well then, why are you here?"

Bored, the girl casually explained she had an argument with her mother and her mother had called the doctor and the doctor decided to put her in the hospital.

"But it says here that you have pneumonia," Donald said incredulously.

"Oh, there's nothing wrong with me; I don't even have a cough."

> *Now back in those days, Benson & Hedges were very expensive cigarettes. So not only was this girl sitting up there, her legs crossed, watching television, and smoking a cigarette, but she was smoking the most expensive cigarette money could buy. And here was this poor, dumb intern (me), running all over the place, working his ass off to take care of a patient who had absolutely nothing wrong with her.*
>
> *I wrote a two sentence note in her chart about the fact that the only complaint she had was that she had an argument with her mother. On Monday morning, after being up for over fifty hours, I had a big to-do with the Chairman of the Department of Medicine. I told him I thought this was a disgusting way to do business, to take advantage of interns. And that they shouldn't be letting people in the hospital like that.*
>
> *He sort of agreed with me, but he decided, then and there, that I was going to be a troublemaker and he didn't invite me back to do my residency at St. Elizabeth's.*

Another man may have taken this as a personal rejection, or at least, convincing evidence that when speaking to a superior, one should keep one's mouth shut. But not Don Wilson. For him, this simply was evidence that St. Elizabeth's was not the right place for him. And rather than seeing it as a rebuff, he looked for and found the silver lining.

> *Not being invited to stay at St. Elizabeth's turned out to be one of the best things that ever happened to me. If I had stayed, I'd probably become a practicing doc somewhere and never would have been motivated to do anything else.*

Instead, Donald ended up landing a position on Maurice Strauss' service at the Veterans Administration Hospital, one of the most coveted medical residencies in all of Boston

The chair of medicine at St. Elizabeth's may have told him "My way or the highway." But instead, Don Wilson, as always, went his own way: straight to the top.

CHAPTER 4

Heeding the Call of Academic Medicine
Blazing a Trail Less Traveled

> ***Would you like to swing on a star***
> *"Swing on a Star," lyrics by*
> Johnny Burke
> Recorded in 1963, Big Dee Irwin
> and Little Eva

    A career in academic medicine was never part of Donald's original thinking. Like most people, he always assumed that "being a doctor" meant settling down someplace agreeable, hanging up a shingle for oneself, and going into clinical practice. But along the way, a brighter star caught Wilson's eye and eventually launched him on a four-decade journey across the nation and around the globe.
    It started in Boston. After surviving a grueling internship at St. Elizabeth's, where his low tolerance for inefficiency had cost him an invitation to return, Donald soon discovered that his residency at the larger, more prestigious Veterans' Affairs Hospital was more than just a step up. Certainly, the hours were far more humane, and the cases were often more complex, and therefore, more interesting. But the real difference at the VA was the people. Here, for the first time in his

professional life, the medical establishment not only acknowledged his presence, many considered him an equal. Among the dozens of gifted physicians walking the halls of Boston's sprawling VA Hospital, Don Wilson had arrived.

Not that the work was easy. Back in the early 1960s, hospitals had no Intensive Care Units for their sickest patients and few laboratory technicians standing by to evaluate blood and perform other tests. As a medical resident, Donald had to do much of his own lab work, there were never enough nurses to go around, and, as usual, there were no African-American physicians to serve as role models or guides. After all, this was 1963, the year four little black girls died in a Birmingham church bombing, the year President John F. Kennedy was shot down in Dallas, and the year ten thousand people marched in Washington, DC, to hear Martin Luther King Jr. tell the nation he had a dream.

As a young, black physician with a brilliant mind and a low tolerance for mediocrity, Donald Wilson, would have to find his own way.

> *I had no mentors during my internship at St. Elizabeth's and few role models at the VA. But that was alright. I never really liked going to people and asking for advice. I find it is almost always wrong.*

Finding Academic Medicine

Back in medical school, Don thought he might pursue a specialty in pediatrics, but the frustrations of dealing with the mothers shifted his interest toward internal medicine, instead. Adults, he reasoned, generally don't show up at the hospital with their emotionally distraught parents screaming at you.

Still, caring for sick adults had its difficult moments, too, especially for a vigilant young doctor who had yet to have his first patient die. No matter how much you know and no matter how hard you work, death sometimes prevails.

The scrawny man in the hospital bed was barely thirty years old, not much older than Donald. He had leukemia, and the plain truth was that the leukemia was winning.

> *He told me he didn't want to die. Every time I'd come in, he'd beg me to save his life. I kept ordering more and more blood transfusions to keep him going, and they did. But there came a point when it just didn't make sense to keep pouring more and more blood into his circulatory system. The Attending Physician made the final decision to discontinue treatment, but I was the one standing there when the poor man finally passed.*

Death was the ultimate enemy and it didn't take long before Donald realized that while clinicians fought the good fight in the trenches everyday, it was the researchers and academics that made any real progress in medicine. There's only so much blood one can pour into the current system, he thought. The only way to get ahead is to expand what we know and teach it effectively to as many doctors as we can. So while most of his peers chose various clinical practices, Donald began paying closer attention to those who were heeding the call of academic medicine.

In 1963, Maurice Strauss was one such man. A brilliant physician and one of the nation's most outstanding medical educators, Straus was legendary at the VA.

"Everyone feared him," recalled Wilson, quickly adding, "I didn't, of course."

Strauss's sharp mind impressed, rather than intimidated Wilson and the two men hit it off from the start. At morning report, the session when residents reported to the chief of medicine about new admissions and any problems from the previous night, Strauss frequently called upon Wilson to answer medical questions. At the beginning of his second year of residency, Strauss selected Wilson to accompany him on rounds to see all patients with liver disease. Ascites, the accumulation of large amounts of fluid within the abdomen, was a special interest of Strauss. The continuing challenge of trying to understand the causes, impacts, and treatments of ascites in patients with chronic liver disease whetted Wilson's curiosity and marked the beginning of his journey into academic medicine.

Rather than limiting him to clinical practice, academic medicine would allow Wilson to pursue a mix of clinical care, teaching, and research. But, as usually, he'd have to blaze his own trail. Back in the 1960s, less than 3% of U.S. physicians were African-American and very few pursued careers in academic medicine. Even today, most minority physicians work in health clinics or set up private clinical practices in urban centers and the rural South. In fact, less than 5% of African-American physicians spend any time teaching or doing research.

Nonetheless, a year after arriving at Boston's VA Hospital in the early 1960s, Wilson not only had set his sights on a career in academic medicine, he was quickly making a name for himself, even among the hospital's most accomplished players.

> *One of the highest compliments ever paid to me was during my residency at the VA. We had weekly rounds with Franz Inglefinger. Now the name Franz Inglefinger probably doesn't mean anything to you, but at the time, he was one of THE outstanding names in gastroenterology. If you had to pick two giants in that field, he would be one of them. He was extraordinarily highly thought of as a clinician.*
>
> *During one of the conferences, they presented one of my patients, while I had been called out for an emergency. Afterwards, the chief resident told me "We discussed your patient and*

Dr. Inglefinger said he had a particular recommendation in mind, but he was unwilling to recommend it because he had heard you didn't think it was the best way to go. He was unwilling to even recommend it until he had a chance to talk to you and see why you didn't want to do it." He respected me that much.

As it turned out I was wrong and he was right, but I was deeply honored that he showed my thinking that level of consideration.

The chief of gastroenterology at the VA was Robert Donaldson, who also impressed Wilson as bright and caring. Indeed, he played a major role in Wilson's decision to choose gastroenterology as his medical specialty. As it turned out when Wilson was ready to become a gastroenterology fellow working with Donaldson, Donaldson left Boston to move to another part of the country. This sequence of events would be repeated several times in Wilson's career, each time to his long-term benefit.

With Donaldson not available, Wilson went to Tufts (his medical school) and the New England Medical Center to seek a fellowship. But the chief of gastroenterology apparently was not interested. Wilson would recall later with some satisfaction that he was able to become a full professor before that chief who had refused to hire him. Thomas Chalmers, one of the world's experts in liver disease did hire Wilson in the combined position of GI fellow and chief resident. Wilson published his first paper in the medical literature with Chalmers in the prestigious *New England Journal of Medicine.*

By the end of his second residency, Wilson had made such an impression that the VA's Chief of Medicine Maurice Strauss eagerly offered him a staff position as Chief of Medical Oncology. Wilson, who had spent the last two years training in GI and liver disease, pointed out that he had little experience in oncology.

"No problem," insisted the Chief of Medicine. "I don't pick training, I pick people, and you are the man I want. It doesn't matter if you're not trained in it; you'll learn it."

An Unexpected Side Trip

But just as Wilson's medical career was about to take off, the Air Force unexpectedly altered his flight pattern. Not only would he have to forgo becoming Chief of Oncology at the VA Hospital, not only would he have to leave Boston to spend what could have been two crushingly boring years in Omaha, Nebraska, now Wilson would be forced, once again, to deal head on with an ugly reality of American life in 1966, a reality that not even his prestigious white coat could deflect.

It seems that, while the United States government was perfectly willing to draft an African-American doctor into the Air Force and ship him off to the Midwest to provide medical care for their upper brass, the local white landlords, who owned most of the rental properties surrounding the base, had an entirely different idea. Wilson could go ahead and save all the big-shots he liked, but they were not about to take rent from a "colored."

So, while the other doctors and their families enjoyed the convenience of living at a new apartment complex near the base, Donald, his wife, and four-year-old son were explicitly not welcome. With no federal housing laws in 1966, the landlord simply said No.

Wilson was livid.

> *I raised hell. I really raised hell. I thought, Here I am, I don't want to be here anyway, but here I am, drafted into the United States military, and you are telling me I'm good enough to take care of you if you are sick, but I'm not good enough to live in your apartments?*

Wilson called his congressman, the Air Force base, the mayor of Omaha, and anyone else who would listen. Long before he arrived, most of the staff at Strategic Air Command (SAC) headquarters were well aware that Donald E. Wilson was coming to town.

In time, the landlord called him back.

"Come on now, Wilson," he said. "You know if I rent to you, I won't be able to fill the rest of my apartments. No one will be willing to live here and I'll end up having to go bankrupt. What will become of me and my family? Besides, you know there is really nothin' you can do about it. There's no law against it."

Donald quickly replied, "There may be no law against it, but there *is* something I can do about it. I'd be willing to bet that most of the people who are renting from you are military personnel, isn't that right?"

The landlord agreed.

"Well, I can fix it so that *no* military person will be able to rent any of your apartments, ever again. Do you think perhaps *that* might make you go bankrupt?"

There was a moment of silence on the other end of the phone. Then the landlord lowered his voice and began to beg, "Please, Dr. Wilson, you can't put me in this position. You can't do this to my wife and kids. What would I do, where would we go?" he whined. "Please, can't we work something out?"

Wilson, well rehearsed in the nuances of negotiation, said nothing.

"I'll tell you what I'm gonna do," continued the landlord. "I've got several private homes in the area, nice homes. How about, for the same rent as the apartment you wanted, I set you up in a nice three-bedroom house? Would that work for you, Dr. Wilson?"

Wilson said nothing.

"How about I give you a brand new refrigerator, too, for your three-bedroom house?"

More silence.

"And a new washer-dryer?"

Still no reply.

"And a brand new television set?" the landlord squirmed. "Please?"

"OK," Wilson finally spoke. "I'll take your three-bedroom house."

The next week, Donald and his family packed up and moved into one of the largest, best-appointed rental homes of any draftee at the airbase.

Finding Meaningful Work

A three-bedroom house was nice, but luxurious accommodations were hardly enough to compensate Donald for having to pass up an important position at the VA. And if being stranded more than twelve hundred miles from Boston with a racist landlord wasn't bad enough, it got worse. Now, after a dozen years of intensely focused effort—after going to Harvard, getting through medical school, surviving St. Elizabeth's, and building a name for himself at the VA—suddenly, there was next to nothing for Don to do. For the first time in his adult life, Donald Wilson had too much time on his hands, and he didn't like it.

> *When they drafted me into the Air Force in 1966, they also drafted three thousand other doctors. At SAC headquarters in Omaha, we had more than one hundred doctors for an eighty-six-bed hospital. There were tons of generals, and there were even more doctors standing by to take care of them. It was ridiculous. We had two neurologists, two ophthalmologists, and several urologists. It was really bad. I can remember one of Air Force ophthalmologists who had absolutely nothing to do. Nothing. He had no opportunity to keep his basic skills up; he just had nothing to do. He kept yelling and complaining about it until they finally transferred him someplace else. We didn't have not enough work for one ophthalmologist, let alone two.*

Heeding the Call of Academic Medicine

Medical office at Offutt Air Force Base, Omaha, NB; 1966

Formal Military dress, USAF 1967

Being a man of action, Don decided to take matters into his own hands. After six months with nearly nothing to do all day, the good doctor set out to find some real work. After making a few phone calls, Wilson met with the chairman of medicine and chief of gastroenterology at the University of Nebraska's medical school.

> *I needed to find something worthwhile, something I could do on the side. So I decided to go down to the University and see how I could help out. They didn't have too many faculty teaching specialties at that time, so I became the person responsible for teaching liver disease to their medical students.*

While most of his fellow draftees lingered restlessly at the base, Wilson went off to make rounds at the university's hospital, as well as at the VA Hospital in Omaha. Instead of killing time while dying of boredom, Donald figured he might as well save a few lives. Like so many of his other choices in a lifetime of big and small accomplishments, to Wilson, this unusual move was really no big deal.

> *What was the point of complaining when there was plenty of work to do? I could have just sat around and enjoyed happy hour at the officers' club every day, but fortunately I found ways to stay active in GI. I found ways to be constructive.*

With the advantage of hindsight, Wilson would later say that his unexpected detour through the Air Force was among the best "wrong turns" of his career.

> *It is very clear to me that if I had not gotten drafted into the Air Force, I probably would have spent my entire life in Massachusetts. It's also very clear that if I had stayed in Massachusetts, I would never be in the position that I'm in now. I watched a number of*

> *my friends stay right there in the Boston area. They stayed in what I call interesting but meaningless jobs.*

The Air Force may have provided the detour that got Wilson out of his geographic comfort zone, but it was Wilson, himself, who found ways to make the most of it. His contributions at the University of Nebraska were noted, so much so that they asked him to stay on as a full-time faculty member at the completion of his military duty.

Still, when the Air Force finally cut him loose in 1968, Donald's first instinct was to pack up his family and dash back to Massachusetts. Once again, fate intervened and, once again, Wilson found a way to turn the unexpected to his advantage.

> *After the Air Force, I was determined to get back to Boston. I had planned to work with Tom Chalmers who had trained me in liver disease at the Lemuel Shattuck Hospital. But then, three or four months before I was to start, he called to tell me he was leaving the hospital and there would be another person in his position, but I should come anyway.*
>
> *That didn't work for me, so I started looking around and a guy at Brooklyn Hospital offered me a position as Associate Chief of Gastroenterology. The title didn't actually mean anything because there were only three of us in the entire division. But the job would allow me to spend some time in the laboratory doing research, in addition to my clinical duties. That appealed to me.*

As soon as Don arrived in New York to take up his first full-time position in academic medicine as Associate Chief of Gastroenterology at Brooklyn Hospital, he began looking in earnest for an area of research in which to make his mark.

As it turned out, he hit a bull's eye.

In the late 1960s, medical research was still in the relatively early stages of understanding how cells work. I worked for a guy named Robert Levine, who was doing research on cyclic AMP, which is like a switch that allows things to go in and out of cells, activating various enzyme systems and biological actions. Levine said there was another compound that was just beginning to get some notoriety called prostaglandins. He thought that might interest me because not much had been done on it yet.

He was right. It took me less than two weeks to read everything in the world ever written about prostaglandins—the entire published literature. So I jumped right in and started doing animal studies on prostaglandins, looking at its effects on gastric secretion, looking at its effects on alcohol-induced liver damage and a variety of other studies. There was so little known about this that in just six months I became a world expert on prostaglandins and the gastrointestinal tract. I became the first person to measure the effect of prostaglandins on acid secretion in man, and many other firsts.

In addition to his leading edge research, Wilson worked as an instructor of medicine at the State University of New York in Brooklyn where he relished his role as an educator. He taught medical students in physical diagnosis and made rounds at University Hospital in Brooklyn. He received an award from the students for his teaching.

But Wilson's many accomplishments, on the wards, in the laboratory, and in the classroom, only made it harder for him to witness the substandard medical care that many minority Americans received. He observed that many physicians didn't really interact with minority patients. The doctors' intellectual capacity to reach a diagnosis was frequently clouded by biases brought into the evaluation, based upon race or social standing. Although he didn't know the data, Wilson felt certain that minorities received less competent medical care and died more frequently from similar diseases than did Caucasians.

All this hit Donald closer to home when his own father became ill.

> *I rushed right back to Worcester when I heard he was in the hospital. As soon as I walked into the room, it was perfectly obvious to me that he had suffered a stroke. He didn't know he had a stroke. Nobody in the hospital knew he had a stroke. In fact, no one in the hospital knew what was going on.*
>
> *My father had a stroke because some little intern or resident found that he had an elevated blood pressure, and decided to lower it. But my father also had a condition called Aortic Insufficiency, and an elevated blood pressure was in part an adaptation to maintain an adequate cerebral and cardiac blood flow. So the idiots lowered his blood pressure precipitously before performing any other studies and he had a stroke. I tried to get him to change doctors, but he wouldn't listen to me. He had the same doctor that had "taken care" of my mother, a doctor who didn't know enough to write his own orders for the house staff. He had to send his patients in and let the residents write up the orders because he wasn't sure what to do. In my opinion, this guy had killed my mother, and now he was killing my father, too. I've had my share of personal experiences with lousy medical care. More than my share.*

The double heartbreak of losing both parents to insensitive, incompetent, and unequal care nagged at Wilson over the years and later played a major role in shaping his career choices.

Making His Mark

Don continued his prostaglandin research at Brooklyn Hospital and his teaching duties at SUNY until 1971. But after three years, he was ready for a change.

Holding Cocoa who lived to be 20 years old, surviving Rockville Centre, NY, Chicago, Il, and Scarsdale, NY: 1969

Levine was leaving to become Chief of Gastroenterology at the State University of New York in Syracuse. He really wanted me to come with him, but that was the last place I wanted to go. Since working in his laboratory at Brooklyn, people were assuming that my work was his work. Even though my name was first on the publications, people assumed it was his work because he had been around longer than I had. He was getting credit for my research and I didn't particularly like that. So I said, No Thanks.

Brooklyn Hospital tried hard to hang onto their rising star. They told him he was a better doctor than his previous boss, and now that Levine had moved on, they were ready to move Don up to Chief of Gastroenterology. But when the salary offer fell significantly short of what Wilson knew they had been paying Levine, and then word got out that they planned to close the animal quarters to save money, all but killing any further prostaglandin research, Wilson decided to take a pass.

They said I was better, but then they offered me less money. Would they have offered me an equal salary if I were white? It's one of those questions that no one can ever answer yet never goes away.

Nevertheless, with his impressive background and rapidly growing stack of cutting-edge research papers, Wilson was quickly offered positions at Columbia University, Yale, and the University of Illinois. To most people's surprise, he chose Illinois. Few could understand why anyone in their right mind would take Illinois over Columbia or Yale. To most people, it just didn't make sense. But for a man blazing his own trail, it made perfect sense.

It was really very simple. If I had gone to Columbia or Yale, I would never be where I am today. At Yale, I would have had little time to do my own research or build my own career. I would have spent all my time seeing patients, and my prostaglandin research would have come to a screeching halt. At Columbia, I could have done some research but the support I was looking for, in terms of research space and the like, just wasn't there.

So in 1971, Wilson turned the big boys down and went off to the University of Illinois in Chicago. Later, he would call it "one of the smartest decisions I ever made," not because the institution was so much better than anywhere else, but because "it put my fate in my own hands."

They gave me a nice suite of laboratories and it was up to me to make something happen, to get funded, if I could do it. It didn't bother me in the least to turn down two big name schools for a lesser institution. I've never been particularly impressed with names. The truth is, the potential for doing well at a "lesser institution" is much greater than at a big-name place. So, off I went, bright-eyed and bushy-tailed to the University of Illinois.

Don had been recruited to Chicago by a gentleman named Morton Bogdonoff, MD, then the chairman of medicine at the University of Illinois. At the time, Bogdonoff had promised him an associate professorship, but when he arrived, the dean decided he "wasn't ready" for that rank and he made Don an Assistant Professor instead. Wilson accepted the disappointment, worked hard, and within two years was tenured and promoted to Associate Professor. And two years after that, he became the youngest full Professor at the University of Illinois School of Medicine.

I had a good time in Chicago. It was a lot of fun. The faculty members were great, the students were appreciative, and the house staff were hard working. Most of the division chiefs were around the same age, so we had a lot of activities in common. My career took off! I became an internationally respected expert on prostaglandins and the GI tract, and the GI program at Illinois grew enormously.

But life wasn't all roses for the young physician on his way up. His wife did not accompany him to Chicago, taking an apartment in Manhattan instead. Donald was left to care for their seven-year-old son. For over a year, Wilson had to get his boy off to school each morning, work all day, run errands on his way home, and take care of his son at night. A year later, Wilson's wife unexpectedly arrived in Chicago. However, the magic was gone and the couple divorced a few years later in 1976.

That wasn't a good time, but in the end it turned out for the best because a couple years later, I married my current wife of nearly thirty years, Patricia, and we have enjoyed a wonderful life and three more wonderful children.

When Wilson first went to the University of Illinois in 1971, he served as chief of Gastroenterology at the University Hospital, but he was not chief of the overall division. When the University needed a new chief for the overall division in 1973 Don knew he was the best man for the job. And he was prepared to quit, if necessary, to prove it.

Wilson in office at University of Illinois; 1971

My assumption was it's got to be me. Who else could they pick? Then I found out they planned to do this national search for the "right candidate." I said fine, go ahead and do your national search. The very next week I took some time off to look at another position. While I was away, Bogdonoff called my home and my wife said, "Oh, gee, he's not here. He's in such-and-such city." When I got back, he said, "I called around to the top people in the country and they told me I already had the best guy for Chief of Gastroenterology right here in front of me. If you want the position, it's yours."

So Donald became the University of Illinois's first African-American Chief of Gastroenterology. He continued to teach, see patients, and make great strides in the laboratory. Within two years, Wilson became *the* internationally recognized expert on prostaglandins. His study on the effects of prostaglandins on gastric acid secretions in man was the first ever publication on the subject. Soon, various pharmaceutical companies started coming to him with funding, asking Wilson to look at the effects of these compounds in animals and then run early studies in man. For a good ten years or so, there wasn't a single prostaglandin analog developed for use in man that hadn't been screened by some basic work in Don's laboratory.

Soon, Wilson was flying around the world, called to speak about his prostaglandin research at medical institutions and symposiums in Germany, Spain, England, Italy, South American, and even Japan. And he became the gastrointestinal editor for the Journal *Prostaglandins,* a position he held for nearly twenty years.

Despite his many travels, along with his teaching and clinical responsibilities, Wilson continued to closely supervise the work of his students and staff to ensure their work lived up to his standards. He learned first hand that it is essential to personally review research being performed in your laboratory.

One of the reasons it is so important to be involved in the laboratory is that you catch errors. You can catch methodology errors or interpretation errors. For example, one time one of my technicians gave me some results of an experiment that looked absolutely wonderful. In fact, they looked too good. I said, "This looks great." And she said, "Oh yeah the curves are wonderful." I said, "Let me see all of the data." When I saw the raw data, it wasn't so wonderful. She sort of decided to reject data that didn't seem to fit the curve. When I put all those results back, there was no positive conclusion that could be drawn from the experiment. If I hadn't been active in the laboratory and had just let that go and written it up, I would have published something that was totally wrong. Six months later, somebody else would have published a report showing that what I had published was totally wrong.

Wilson on one of many foreign speaking engagements: (Portugal); 1985

Juggling his roles as a top-notch clinician, full Professor, world renowned researcher was never easy. It took long hours, focused attention to details, and sustained hard work.

> *I marvel today at how medical school faculty expect to have all this free time to do research. Folks seem to feel if they don't have 80 percent of their time free to do and think about their research, they can't do any research at all.*
>
> *For me, it was always been a matter of just doing it, of just getting it done. As an assistant professor, I spent six months of the year making rounds. Today, faculty members think it's an outrage if you ask them to do two. I also did another four months a year of GI subspecialty rounds, and in my "spare time" I did research and I did it well enough to get funded. My first grant proposal in my first year at Chicago was rejected. So I fixed it up, resubmitted it, and I was funded every year since. You can't work forty or fifty hours a week and expect to get anywhere.*
>
> *However, if you choose to take such a route, working seventy or more hours a week, you need to be certain that you spouse shares your vision and commitment. There is definitely less time for your family.*

Wilson's tireless dedication paid off. By 1975, Wilson was a full professor, a departmental section chief at a major university, and the world's leading authority in his area of research, with his name on more published papers, awards, and accomplishments than most doctors can brag about when they retire.

He was thirty-eight.

Back to Brooklyn

A year later, in 1976, Wilson was asked to serve as interim chairman of the department of medicine, and he agreed to do so with the proviso that it would not interfere with his scheduled sabbatical the following year. Bogdonoff, at this point, had moved to New York. About two months before his scheduled departure, Wilson met with the executive dean of the college of medicine.

> *I asked the executive dean if he had decided who would be the next chairman, and he said No, that he hoped I would continue to do the job or consider doing it permanently. When I asked him if I could take the permanent job, but still go on sabbatical for six months, he said No. I, therefore, informed him that I would be pleased to continue to do the job for another two months. Two weeks later, he announced that a permanent chair had been selected, one of my colleagues.*

Wilson and wife Patricia attending Royal Ascot, London England in full traditional dress with Liberian Ambassador to the U.K. Herbert Brewer and wife Elizabeth during Wilson's sabbatical: 1978

After taking a year's sabbatical in England to conduct prostaglandin research at Kings College Hospital, University of London, Wilson returned to Chicago in 1978, ready to roll up his sleeves and get back to work. But somehow the environment at the University of Illinois had changed.

> *I returned to Chicago with every intention of staying, but then I learned something that got me thinking. At Illinois, you get elected to serve in positions of authority like the executive committee of the medical school and the academic council for the entire university. You have these positions automatically if you are a chairman of a department, but when I returned from England I was no longer the chairman of a department, so the faculty had to elect me. I discovered that the Chairman of Medicine was trying to tell the faculty how to vote. I don't think he was too excited about having me sitting at the same level he was at. The faculty totally ignored him and elected me anyway, but I found this very disconcerting. I thought, maybe after eight years here, it's time to move on.*

As soon as Wilson let it be known that he was open to looking at other positions, the State University of New York asked if he would consider returning to their Downstate campus in Brooklyn, this time as Chairman of Medicine. At first, the prospect of taking charge of a medical school's most powerful department intrigued him. But after months of frustration with SUNY's inability to come to a final decision and make an offer, Don decided to call the chairman of their search committee and withdraw his name from consideration.

Once again, something unexpected changed his mind.

Just as Wilson was about to tell the head of the search committee to forget the whole thing, the man called and candidly said, "You know,

I want to tell you something that is very disturbing to me. There are a lot of people here who don't want you to come. They just don't want a black man in this job and they're trying to find some way to block your candidacy."

Irritated, but not entirely surprised, Wilson let him go on. "One person told the search committee that he had spoken to the Vice Chancellor at Illinois and she said you were 'very immature.'"

Wilson shoulders stiffened a bit as the man continued. "That didn't set right with me, so I called the Vice Chancellor, myself. She insisted she said nothing of the kind. What she said was that 'Don has done so well for himself and he is so young for such a senior position.' She never said you were immature. Quite the opposite, she said you are very mature."

Wilson smiled at his refreshing candor and resourcefulness, and wondered if perhaps being from Poland might have made it easier for this man to call it racism when he saw it.

"You know something?" Wilson said lightheartedly. "I had originally called to tell you to pull my name from your search. But, you know what? Now you have really pissed me off. I'm starting to think you all deserve me back there."

The two men laughed. A few weeks later, the job was offered and Wilson took it. In time, even those who had resisted his candidacy were glad he came.

> *A year after I was hired, I found out that the acting president at the time really didn't want me to come. In fact, when the search committee narrowed the choice to me, he began calling around the country to see if anyone else wanted the job—even after receiving 142 applications. I didn't know anything about that until he came to my office one day, after he had finally quit his position, and said "I just want you to know that the only*

> *worthwhile thing I did as acting president was to recruit you as chair of medicine. At first, I really didn't think it was a good idea. But I just want you to know that bringing you here is the single accomplishment about which I am the most proud."*
>
> *Well, as it turned out, he did nothing of the kind. Since he was the acting president, the search committee had him handcuffed. Instead of giving him the usual three names, they gave him only one name: mine. Apparently, now he wanted credit for it.*

As chairman of medicine at Downstate, a rare position of power for an African-American physician at a predominantly white institution, Wilson ran the largest department in the medical school and had authority over hundreds of people. He directly supervised the work of thirteen subspecialty divisions, handled the internal medicine training program, and taught internal medicine to medical students.

When Wilson arrived at Downstate, nearly every medical resident and intern working in their hospital had graduated from foreign medical schools. Not one of Downstate's own two hundred plus medical school graduates stayed on for their internships or residencies in medicine, even though Downstate offered the largest medical training program in New York and the second largest in the nation.

That seemed ridiculous to Wilson, but apparently it was just fine with others on campus.

> *I remember someone saying to me over a few drinks at one of those dinners they take you to during the early recruitment process that "Downstate is where the WASPS hire the Jews to take care of the Blacks."*

Now, Wilson set out to change that. Along with his many other duties as Chairman of Medicine, Wilson found ways to make the faculty teach more, spend more time with patients, and be more accountable to the house staff. He also established an open-door policy for all students and house staff, and made it known that they were important to the department.

In time, his efforts paid off. Back in 1980, when Wilson first arrived at Downstate, there was only one other African-American faculty member in the department of medicine and only foreign medical school graduates working as interns or residents. In less than a decade, Wilson recruited more minority faculty and interns, and more women, dramatically boosting the demography of their medical training program to 85 % U.S. graduates. Wilson also changed the complexion of the department of medicine and house staff by selecting quality first. And he continued to recruit extraordinarily talented foreign-trained physicians, many of whom knew more medicine than the faculty who were teaching them.

But despite these gratifying changes, Donald missed the vibrancy of a more active research environment, and in time, began to tire of a campus with so little gumption to grow.

> *At that time, there wasn't an awful lot of research going on at the State University of New York. One of the problems was that the faculty was almost completely supported by state dollars. That meant, no matter what they did, they were going to get paid. There was little incentive to go out and get grants, and for the most part, they didn't. Plus, there was a union, a faculty union, which meant the administration couldn't get anything done.*

Wilson receiving Child Advocate of The Year Award from borough of Brooklyn, NY; 1986

After ten years of this, Wilson grew increasingly restless. The problem was not a lack of work to do, nor a lack of respect from his peers and superiors. In fact, above and beyond Wilson's duties as chairman of medicine, he was also often called upon to help the school make key administrative decisions and to solve knotty administrative problems. The more problems he solved, the more they counted on him to bail them out. It eventually got to the point where the institution seemed to have a hard time deciding what to do about just almost anything without first coming to Don Wilson to get his take on this or that, or his opinion on the latest campus controversy, or his recommendations about what ought to be done.

> *After a while, I felt like I was the only person with any vision for the place, the only person who would stand up for academic*

medicine. The reality was that I was behaving a lot more like a dean than a department chair. And then one day, it occurred to me: If I'm going to act like a dean, I might as well be a dean.

And a few months later, he was gone.

CHAPTER 5

Maryland Meets It's Match
The First African-American Dean of a Majority Medical School

The best is yet to come
"The Best is Yet to Come"
Lyrics by Carolyn Leigh

After ten years at SUNY Downstate, Donald Wilson was ready to get out, go some place new, and be dean. He was ready to find a medical school with growth potential where he could jump in, systematically tackle the problems, and drive the school to the top of the charts.

The only question was, which medical school was ready for him?

Medical school dean jobs are not exactly easy to come by, even though a dozen or more of the nation's 125 accredited allopathic medical schools, at any given time, are actively looking for new deans. With hundreds of physicians and faculty members eager to make the big move to the dean's office, the competition is extraordinary. And of course, there was that other inescapable reality of American medical education prior to 1991: No majority medical school had ever invited an African-American to sit behind the dean's desk. Not even one.

With no deanship offers on the table, Wilson was open to other options. So when the U.S. Department of Health and Human Services called to ask if he'd like to come to Washington, DC, to serve as a senior consultant to the Agency for Health Care Policy and Research, Donald jumped at the chance to try something new. True, the work wasn't especially exciting, but having his expertise personally request by the Secretary of HHS earned Wilson tremendous respect within the agency. Plus, it got him temporarily out of Brooklyn.

During this sabbatical, Wilson cemented his commitment to addressing the nation's disparities in health care and medical training. Given ready access to the raw data, the conclusions were inescapable and depressing. Race was a major factor in determining who was more likely to suffer certain health problems, such as heart disease and cancer. Moreover, race impacted the likelihood of receiving adequate and timely medical treatment for such diseases, with African Americans consistently coming in last place. As a consultant to the department of Health and Human Services, Donald hoped to exert some influence on national policies that might help reverse this trend, or least raise interest in the issue.

An Invitation from Maryland ... Sort of

While at HHS, Wilson received a solicitation from one of the few African-American faculty members at the University of Maryland School of Medicine, urging him to submit his name to their search committee for dean. The request seemed a bit odd, considering that while Wilson was still at SUNY in 1988 this same faculty member had asked him to apply for the dean's position at Maryland before. Wilson had done so, been interviewed, and never heard anything more. Months later Wilson learned that Maryland's dean search had been aborted, but no one bothered to inform him.

> *Unfortunately, the person who chaired the search committee never had the decency to write or call me to say the search had been discontinued. I simply never heard from him again.*

Turned off by his prior experience, but curious to see what might develop from this latest invitation, once again Wilson sent in his curriculum vitae. And once again, months went by and he heard nothing back.

Still, the prospect was intriguing. Wilson knew that the University of Maryland School of Medicine in Baltimore was one of the oldest public medical colleges in the nation. From a small group of physicians teaching a handful of students in their homes at the turn of the 19th century, the medical school was now part of a sprawling fifty-acre complex at the University of Maryland, Baltimore that anchored the west side of the city. The medical school had grown from a single building in 1812 to a three-building complex in 1991.

Wilson also knew that Maryland's medical school ranking had fallen and the school's reputation was sagging as large sections of the campus seemed to be dozing in the shadow of the mighty Johns Hopkins University Medical School, flexing its muscle on the east side of town. While some stellar clinicians and researchers continued to make significant breakthroughs and important achievements at Maryland, many other faculty simply sat on the sidelines while their Hopkins counterparts aggressively pursued and often won the big research grants.

Such a gloomy scene might have turned others away. But for Wilson that was "the real beauty" of the place, he said. "There was so much room for improvement, so many opportunities to grow. I knew I could have a real impact."

Improving and growing, after all, was exactly what Maryland's medical school had been doing for most of its long and famous history.

Back in the country's colonial days, medical treatments were more likely to be administered by a barber or apothecary owner than by someone educated in medical science. Apprenticeships, rather than a formal system of medical education, were the norm. The causes of diseases were largely unknown, and physicians were often considered quacks.

One of those "quacks" turned out to be the famous John B. Davidge, a native of Annapolis who earned his medical degree at Glasgow

University in Scotland in 1793 and practiced medicine in England for several years before returning to Maryland. In 1801, Davidge joined a handful of attending physicians at the newly established Baltimore General Dispensary, Baltimore's first hospital. With no formal medical school from which to draw new physicians, Davidge and the other doctors offered lectures to interested students in their homes. When more room was needed, Davidge and a colleague ran a notice in the local newspaper, announcing that a new anatomy course would be offered in a building Davidge owned near the center of town. More than once, when word got out that cadavers were being dissected, angry mobs stormed the lessons, scaring off the students and trashing the building.

It was, in fact, this fierce community objection to the study of human anatomy in Baltimore that drove Davidge to ask the Maryland state legislature to formally incorporate a medical school, protected by the aegis of the state. On December 18, 1807, the College of Medicine of Maryland was founded, with Davidge and five others serving as its first faculty. The school became the fifth oldest surviving formal college of medicine established in the United States, and the first in the South.

Soon after, as a direct outgrowth of the new medical school, the state assembly charted the University of Maryland in 1812. More than a century later in 1920, the professional schools on the Baltimore campus—including medicine, dentistry, pharmacy, nursing, social work, and law—merged with the Maryland State College of Agriculture in College Park to form the precursor of today's University System of Maryland, now with eleven campuses throughout the state.

From the very start, the faculty of Maryland's College of Medicine insisted on inclusion. The school's original bill of incorporation stated that the new institution…

> *shall be founded and maintained forever upon a most liberal plan, for the benefit of students of every religious denomination, who shall be freely admitted to equal privileges, and advantages*

of education, and to all the honors of the College, according to their merit, without requiring or enforcing any religious or civil tests.

The school's commitment to religious tolerance, however, did not apply to race and it took until 1951 before the first black student was admitted. Maryland's School of Medicine was so adamant about keeping blacks out that the state preferred to pay the tuition of any qualified African American student to attend a medical school elsewhere.

Back in 1809, just ten students registered for the first official class, five of whom earned their medical degrees in April 1810. At first, the new College of Medicine, as it was called, functioned with no buildings, no text books, and no equipment. Teachers held classes in their own homes, lecturing to students who had purchased cards of admission. In time, the faculty pooled enough money to buy from Revolutionary War hero John Eager Howard a tract of land on what is now the northeast corner of Baltimore's Lombard and Greene Streets.

In 1811, the cornerstone was laid for the famous Davidge Hall, the nation's oldest building in continuous use for medical education. The three-story stone building featured a circular theater for the observation of surgery, a chemistry hall, a library, and several dissection rooms, complete with secret stairways and hidden exits for students and faculty to escape the occasional angry mob.

Undaunted by the local anti-dissection sentiment, Maryland's College of Medicine became the first school in the country to build a teaching hospital in 1823, providing clinical access and hands-on instruction for medical students. Modeled after Edinburgh and Glasgow, The Infirmary in Baltimore provided a large operating amphitheater and beds for as many as sixty patients. Alongside experienced physicians, medical students took case histories and followed patients through their treatments and recovery, laying the early groundwork for yet another Maryland first: the country's first medical residency training program.

By 1825 the medical college had more than three hundred students from nearly every state in the nation. At first, The Infirmary, which later become University of Maryland Hospital, was financed and run entirely by the medical school faculty. Later, the state wrestled control away from the faculty and created a board of trustees to run the hospital. Eventually the situation was adjudicated and some autonomy was returned to the faculty. But continued squabbling over ownership and authority went on for decades as The Infirmary struggled through years of under-financing and over-crowding, especially when large number of sailors flooded into Baltimore's port, ill with yellow fever.

With physician dedication and some state funds, the hospital persisted during the mid-1800s, growing big enough and stable enough to meet the crushing medical demands of the Civil War. After the war, student enrollment grew and the hospital expanded to accommodate more than twelve hundred inpatients and fifteen thousand outpatients, yearly, by 1880. As the nation approached the turn of the nineteenth century, The Infirmary medical staff, who also served as faculty for the school, increasingly applied a systematic, scientific approach to their work. Their far-reaching accomplishments spanned many disciplines, impacting the understanding and practice of medicine worldwide. More sophisticated fund raising allowed for continued expansion of the hospital and medical school, with modernized clinics and laboratories. Flourishing specialties attracted top practitioners and professors. New buildings were constructed, and by 1934, Maryland's College of Medicine erected the country's first medical skyscrapers.

In 1983 University Hospital, which continued to be plagued by annual budget deficits, insufficient funds for expansion, and inclusion under a myriad of state regulations, was spun off as a separate private non-for-profit corporation. This new institution, with its own board of directors, became the University of Maryland Medical System. Now free from the University of Maryland, the new hospital pursued its own course. However, to maintain its academic commitment, the legislature required that the new hospital's medical staff consist only of medical school faculty, and further, that the medical school's dean, University of Maryland chancellor and president, and several members of the board of regents sit as members of the corporation's board.

Among the brightest stars in the Maryland medical constellation is the renowned Shock Trauma Center. Founded in 1969 by surgeon R Adams Cowley on the idea that expert care in the first "golden hour" after traumatic injury could dramatically save lives, the center spawned a statewide emergency rescue helicopter transportation system and quickly became the nation's gold standard in emergency medical care. In 1989, Maryland's Shock Trauma Center opened the doors of the world's first stand alone trauma center, with its own building and rooftop heliport.

But despite so many "firsts" and stunning accomplishments, Maryland's medical school and hospital was also operating under the ever-growing shadow of another great medical institution on the rise in Baltimore, the Johns Hopkins School of Medicine and Hospital. Opening four years after the Hopkins Hospital was established in 1889, their new medical school quickly flourished with generous private endowments and outstanding faculty. In 1910, when educator Alexander Flexner (a Johns Hopkins University graduate) reported to the Carnegie Institute on the status of the nation's medical education, he recommended that all other medical schools in the state of Maryland be shut down and their resources turned over to Hopkins. While Flexner's ridiculous advice was completely ignored, the mantle of Maryland's second-class status was not so easily shrugged off.

In fact, by the time Donald Wilson was considering the dean's job in 1990, some University of Maryland faculty seemed intimidated, if not downright demoralized by their cross-town neighbor, declining, for example, to compete for research grants if they suspected someone at Hopkins was applying for the same funds.

Wilson was also aware that, despite the school's early commitments to religious justice, Maryland's medical school faculty and student body included only a tiny sprinkling of African-Americans. The school had no black faculty prior to 1952, when Ernest Brown became their first

African-American surgical resident. In 1956, African-American student enrollment went up a whopping 200%, bringing the grand total to four. A year later, the hospital had three black residents in 1957, one in obstetrics/gynecology and two in psychiatry.

While their numbers remained dismally low, their achievements were considerable, with some of Maryland's African-American faculty gaining worldwide recognition for their accomplishments. Elijah Saunders, for example, after earning his medical degree from the school and becoming their first African-American resident in internal medicine in 1960, went on to be recognized as a leading expert in the study and treatment of hypertension in people of African descent.

Tyson Tilden, also African-American, joined the University of Maryland School of Medicine's Department of Pediatrics in 1968. A respected teacher and researcher, Tilden helped established the Division of Pediatric Research. He also gave quite generously of his time and service to the greater Baltimore community, including chairmanship of the Baltimore City Public School's Board of Commissioners, where he worked tirelessly to improve the classroom experience for all city children.

But over the years, despite multi-tasking superstars like Tilden and Saunders, the numbers of African-American medical school faculty and students remained dismally low. Even in Baltimore, a city where more than 70 percent of the residents were non-white, minorities accounted for only 8% of the University of Maryland School of Medicine's student body in 1990.

So when Wilson ran into Elijah Saunders at a scientific meeting and Saunders suggested that Wilson resubmit his CV for the dean's job at Maryland, Wilson was more than a little surprised.

"Are you joking?" Wilson quipped. "I dealt with these people before and they didn't even give me the courtesy of responding. So, no, I am not particularly interested in the job."

Saunders, one of Maryland's few African-American faculty and, at the time, the only African-American in the school's powerful Department of Medicine, said, "Well, it's different now."

Different? Wilson was unconvinced. But Saunders was insisting and he figured there was no harm in sending in his CV, yet again.

Four months later, Donald ran into Saunders. "Wilson, I thought you said you were going to send in your CV?"

"I did!"

"Really? I asked the search committee and they said they never got it."

"Well, isn't that interesting," Wilson mused. "The post office never sent it back to me, so I have to assume they received it. I told you this would go nowhere."

Saunders thought for a moment. "Do me a favor," he said. "Send a copy of your CV to my office and I'll hand deliver it to the search committee, myself."

But when Saunders tried to give them Wilson's impressive CV, the search committee would have nothing of it. They told him, again, that they "never received it," and besides, the search was now officially closed. They simply weren't taking any more CV's.

Rounding Up the Troops

Livid, Saunders rounded up a tiny group of vocal African-American faculty and went immediately to the campus president. Among them, was the late Tyson Tilden.

"The first time I met Don Wilson, I was impressed—no—make that blown away," recalled Tilden. "I interviewed him during our first search process, and I found him to be a very strong candidate. His answers to my questions were all very thorough, very complete. But even more than his answers, what particularly impressed me about Don Wilson were his questions for me. He had about thirty or forty of them, everything from history to academia to the Baltimore business climate. Across the country, medicine was changing very rapidly and Wilson clearly was thinking ahead. I've interviewed many, many candidates in my time, for all kinds of positions. This man was at the very top of the chart."

After listening to Tilden and the others, the acting campus president said he would instruct the medical school search committee to take a serious look at Donald Wilson.

> *And then they were caught. My CV was as good as, or better than anyone else's under consideration. The search committee had no choice but to interview me. At that point, there was nothing they could say but, "Yeah, he's a credible candidate." As it turns out, I became one of their major candidates.*

But the battle was far from over. The quiet truth was, some people at the University just couldn't see an African-American sitting behind the dean's desk, no matter how wonderful his qualifications. In fact, if the University of Maryland at Baltimore didn't already have a big, bad, racial-tinged public relations problem on its hands, they may have been able to keep Wilson out of serious consideration altogether. Ironically, it was Maryland's own previous, good-old-boy, backroom maneuvering that had painted them into a corner and inadvertently helped opened their doors to real change.

As luck would have it, just the year before the university had asked world-renowned spinal cord expert, Harvard professor Dr. Augustus White, an African-American, to serve as its campus president. The *Washington Post* called it a "stellar choice" for the University. In private, however, not everyone was equally thrilled. In fact, just prior to White's arrival, a big organizational shake up was secretly planned that would significantly limit the scope of White's power on the Baltimore campus. Specifically, the Board of Regents decided at the last minute to downgrade White's job by pulling the Law School out of his jurisdiction, a move that many saw as racially motivated.

Maryland Meets It's Match

Making matters worse, no one bothered to tell White about this important and insulting change in his job description until just hours before his press conference to announce his acceptance. Angered by what he and others viewed as a sneak attack, White used the press conference as a public forum to tell the University of Maryland exactly what they could do with their bloody job.

That left the campus with no president and a fresh batch of racist mud on its predominately white face. So, less than a year later, when the medical school reopened its search for a new dean, it couldn't hurt to throw the name of an accomplished black physician, such as Donald Wilson, into the mix at the last minute—as long as it didn't actually go anywhere. Publicly, they could say, "See how progressive we are," while, privately, some members of the search committee made disparaging remarks about Wilson during the selection process.

> *It got back to me that the guy who had chaired the previous search committee in 1988, the one who never called me back to say the search had been called off, had been making some comments about me during the second search. He said in that old Southern drawl of his: "Well, Wilson has done fine for himself—for a black man. But he's not for our medical school."*
>
> *I found out that even one my strongest eventual supporters, a member of the hospital leadership team said "It's not the right time for a black dean." When someone asked him exactly when would it be the right time, he said when there are more black faculty who can support him. When they asked him how did he think that might happen, and who exactly was going to recruit all these new black faculty, he just said "It'll happen in its time and that time is not now."*

Nonetheless, Wilson's stunning qualifications made it very difficult for the search committee to entirely remove him from consideration.

Instead, when they finally narrowed their search to a short list of four names, they put Wilson (the only African-American) safely into the number three slot.

That should have been enough to keep Wilson out of the dean's office while still creating the impression that a black man was being seriously considered—except for one tiny little detail. Again, a bit of luck intervened. It turned out that the acting president, the man who was just handed that short list of four names and who was about to select the next dean of the medical school, happened to be a *dentist*.

You see, at Maryland, the dental school had always been in the shadow of the much larger and more powerful School of Medicine. Even worse, at that time, the medical school dean also had the imperial-sounding title of Vice Chancellor. It's hard to imagine any dentist being too fond of that. So when dental school dean Errol Reese was asked to fill the gap left by Gus White and take over as president for the campus while the medical school searched for a new dean, the dentist finally had his day. For the first time, a dental school dean was going to exert some real power over the school that some called the "eight-hundred-pound gorilla."

The medical school handed president Reese their short list of four names, ranked in order of their preference. And the dental-school-dean-turned-president promptly bid them all a nonverbal "get lost" by immediately disposing of their first two picks. That left Wilson, whom the medical school search committee had safely tucked away as their number three guy, in first place, with another gentleman as the new number two.

> *I had no idea about any of this at the time. You know, around here, everything is a supposed to be a secret, but sooner or later, you always find out. If Reese hadn't been dean of the dental school, who knows how it might have went.*

President Reese met with the two remaining candidates. Right from the start, there was something about Errol Reese that made Wilson's hair bristle.

> *He seemed to be a nice enough guy, but he appeared to be long on style and short on substance. I wasn't sure I could trust him.*

Reese told Wilson he didn't take long to make decisions and would soon announce the name of the new medical school dean. Two months went by and, once again, Wilson heard nothing.

> *I said, "This is getting ridiculous." I was starting to have some real misgivings about the president's personality and my ability to interact with him. I thought about the comments made by some members of the search committee and I thought to myself, this is a school with a racist history and a lot of in-breeding. Is this really someplace I want to be?*

Back in Brooklyn, Donald began to seriously question whether the Maryland job was worth all this aggravation. If Maryland didn't think it was ready for a black dean, well, perhaps it wasn't.

> *I called Tyson Tilden and I told him I was withdrawing. I said I just don't think I can work with this president. Your institution is just not ready for an African-American dean. There's just too much stuff going on. Tyson said he was disappointed but he understood. We hung up and I assumed that was the end of it.*

It wasn't.

Tyson Tilden, having been at the University of Maryland School of Medicine for more than two decades, understood better than most that the school needed new leadership, *real* leadership. He knew the school needed an individual who could think big and act big, a man who wasn't afraid of challenging the status quo, a man who could bring out the best in people, demand excellence, and lead the school into the new millennium.

"And if such a person also happened to be a brilliant African-American with a CV that could knock your socks off," Tilden figured, "well, so much the better!"

This one, Tilden thought to himself as he hung up the phone, *is not getting away.* As soon as his fingers could get a dial tone, Tilden set to work, calling every influential black man and women he knew in the City of Baltimore—and he knew quite a few. People like legislative committee chairman Pete Rawlings, Dr. Anne Emery, Dr. Roland Smoot, Dr. Sidney Burnett, and others.

Tilden quickly summed up the situation, gave each of them Wilson's New York telephone number, and told them to start calling immediately with reasons why the man *had* to come to Baltimore and be dean. Then he asked his wife to quickly pull together a list and call Wilson with info about homes in the area his family could buy or rent. He even got Baltimore mayor Kurt L. Schmoke to call and ask—no, *beg*—Wilson to change his mind.

Tyson Tilden's orders went out over the Baltimore telephone lines and within minutes, like airplanes stacked up over the airport, the calls started pouring into Brooklyn, landing one after the other on Wilson's office telephone. As soon as one call ended, his phone was ringing again. The calls were short and to the point, with each caller taking a slightly different approach to roughly the same message:

- "I know it looks bad, but this really could be the best place for you."
- "There's real potential here. Baltimore is fertile ground. Pull out some weeds, water it, and it will grow."
- "The system is in a transitional position with the state. We need someone who can work with that."

- "You won't be in it alone; we'll support you every way we can."
- "Wilson, you can't be serious about turning us down!"
- "Think about your place in history, Dr. Wilson. You'll be the first African-American dean of a majority medical school. Not just this year, but for the rest of eternity. Besides, we really need you here."
- "*Please?* Just promise you'll think about it."

The Maryland calls were relentless, reflects Wilson.

> *Over the course of an hour or so, every time I put down the phone, there was someone else from Baltimore, waiting on the line to try to talk me into taking the job. It was really getting ridiculous. I thought, "A man can't get a thing done around here with all these people calling!" I told my secretary to hold the rest of my calls so I could get back to work.*

But the papers on Wilson's desk could no longer hold his attention. Pensive, Donald sat back in his chair and stared blankly at the wall.

Baltimore? he asked himself silently, mulling over the difficult future he certainly would face at the helm of a mediocre and obviously still racist medical school, full of people who had apparently grown quite comfortable with the status quo, even if it didn't come with much status. A man could really get himself in a pile of trouble in a place like that, especially with a campus president who might just as soon not see much get done, especially by a black man in a white coat.

Dean Wilson, he pondered. Sounded OK, but what kind of hornet's nest would that title come with? The place was going to need a lot of work. A lot. Plus, the budget was drying up.

Three minutes passed, then seven minutes, then ten. Finally, Wilson picked up the phone and called Tilden.

"OK," he said. "I'll do it."

Wilson's Way

A week later, the dentist-turned-campus-president called and offered Wilson the job.

"I had no illusions it would be easy."

As it turns out, he was right.

Ironically, each of the other three candidates recommended by the search committee went on to become deans elsewhere. However, their top two choices had short tenures, one only about a year.

CHAPTER 6

A Different Kind of Dean
Less Like a Chairman of the Board, More Like the CEO

You've got to ac-cent-chu-ate the positive
Eliminate the negative
Latch onto the affirmative
And don't mess with Mister In-Between

You've got to spread joy up to the maximum
Bring gloom down to the minimum
Have faith, or pandemonium
Liable to walk upon the scene
          "Accentuate the Positive"
          By Johnny Mercer and Harold Arlen

In the early morning heat of September 3, 1991, Donald Wilson made his way through the already steamy streets of Baltimore in one of the final suffocating days of the city's hottest summer on record. With the University of Maryland gasping under the weight of the worst budget cuts in years and the School of Medicine experiencing a freefall in both money and morale, the doctor knew on his first day as dean that if his new patient was to survive and thrive into the new millennium, he would have to do more than merely stop the bleeding. He would have to build a powerhouse of leading-edge scientific research, innovative medical education, and exemplary clinical care.

But first, the bleeding.

The cuts were massive. Nationally, the state ranked in the bottom 20 percent of states in public support for higher education. Just prior to Wilson's arrival, more than $1.5 million had been carved away from the medical school's $32 million state budget, and additional cuts were just weeks away. Lacking a consistently strong leader at its helm, and with its coffers repeatedly raided as money shifted behind closed doors in a mad scramble to preserve other campus programs and positions, the School of Medicine was losing big.

Anxiety about finances had gotten so bad that, although he wasn't supposed to start until January 1992, the cries for help kept coming from the school until Wilson agreed to leave Brooklyn early and take charge at Maryland four months ahead of schedule. Apparently, after decades of chronic mediocrity, combined with the recent bout of acute budget cuts, the patient could wait no longer.

Leaving behind his wife and family in New York, Wilson hastily moved a few pieces of furniture and some boxes into an apartment on Baltimore's West Lombard Street on Labor Day. The next morning, the humidity already thick, Wilson walked the grimy three and a half blocks to the medical school's Bressler Research Building and rode the elevator alone at dawn to the top floor.

There, in the quiet, well-chilled suite of offices on the 14th floor, with its panoramic views of the steamy city behind air-conditioned glass, Wilson knew he had a choice: He could cool his heals, sit behind the big fancy dean's desk and try to look busy, or he could actually get something done.

In truth, no one would have known the difference. He could easily have simply sat there, picking his way through the huge stacks of papers and unopened mail, meeting with the dozens of people vying to talk to the new man in charge. Who would have known if he merely busied himself with the countless daily duties of being dean, working with what he could within the boundaries of the school's dwindling budget, simply meeting and greeting whomever he was scheduled to meet and greet next, nodding in passive agreement with the powerful department chairs? Who would have known he could have done more, that the school could have done more?

Certainly, no one expected more. Wilson, whose life had been defined by pursuing and often achieving excellence, looked around him and saw a school apparently satisfied to be second-rate. He saw a school essentially run by the departments, with department chairs jealously protecting their individual fiefdoms, and no strong leadership at the top. He saw a school that had been coasting for so many years on autopilot that few people even noticed that no single person held forth a unified vision for the institution, that no single leader was articulating and coordinating, no less achieving, real institutional goals.

Wilson saw an under performing state school, dozing in the shadows of the perennially prosperous Johns Hopkins University, which was busily expanding it's already huge medical campus just a few miles away.

"Dumps Ville, Incorporated" is how one national figure in academic medicine privately characterized Maryland when Wilson agreed to be dean. Tyson Tilden, always the gentleman, put it a bit more kindly, calling the place "a bit sleepy."

So who in the world would have known better if the brand new dean, fresh from New York, who was called in early to keep the school afloat during a fiscal crisis, simply chose to let his lethargic patient sleep?

The truth was, no one would know. No one except Don Wilson.

> *The best thing about coming into a place where everything needs so much work is that there's a lot you can do to improve things, there's so much room to grow. I looked around at this place and where most people saw the status quo, I saw the future. Maryland was a diamond in the rough that just needed proper structuring and polishing.*

Within the dozing school, Wilson saw pockets of wide-awake, top-notch scientists, like Tilden and others, doing rigorous, first-class research. And even though the school was ranked nationally near the bottom third of public medical schools, and even though the school faced the real possibility of losing its accreditation by the powerful Liaison Committee on Medical Education, Wilson saw other real possibilities, as well. From his expansive view from the 14th floor, Wilson looked out at the downtown Baltimore campus and envisioned brand new buildings going up, brand new research equipment rolling in, more and better teaching technologies, newly designed courses for students, more frequent and bigger research grants, stronger faculty, greater community involvement, and a growing, vibrant, cutting-edge medical institution that would help set the standards for medical research, education, and patient care in the 21st century and beyond.

Of course, closing in around this fine, new vision of future excellence, he also saw the state repeatedly slashing the school's current operating budget on one side, and the looming specter of managed care choking off cash flow on the other.

Back in 1991, managed care's penetration into medicine was greater in Maryland than in most other states. Nationally, managed care grew in response to rapidly increasing medical care cost in the last half of the twentieth century. The high costs of remarkable, new technologies, coupled with a no-limits attitude on the part of consumers while most employers footed their health insurance bill, combined to drive the price of medicine up a whopping 14% in one year.

Resources, however, were not limitless and eventually something had to give. At first, the idea of controlling medical costs with managed care was fiercely resisted by the American Medical Association and other professional groups, which had stood firm for decades on the advantages of a fee-for-service system rather than corporately coordinated medical care with a maximum or "capitated" rate per individual. But by 1991, with medical costs rising rapidly, managed care had won over many employers who purchased health insurance for their employees, and most health care providers had little choice but to take what they could get.

The University of Maryland School of Medicine was hit especially hard because the school's total budget was (and still is) partially subsidized by its Practice Plan, the clinical services faculty provided the community. As managed care payers ratcheted down their reimbursement for medical services, the school received less and less money for salaries, research, development, and other costs partially supported by the Practice Plan. Hammered by continuing budgets cuts and the growing pressures of managed care, money at the University of Maryland School of Medicine in the early 1990s was tight. Damn tight.

Southern Exposure

If shrinking funds and low expectations weren't enough to dissuade Wilson from his ambitious visions for transforming the school, there was one more thorny issue quietly at play: This was, after all, *Baltimore*. As a local waitress so succinctly summed it up to a recently transplanted New Yorker as he finished a lonely meal at the Double-T Dinner just west of the city line, "Don't ever forget this is Balmer, Hon. You can dress it up any way you like, but it's still The South."

While the country, as a whole, still had and has a long way to go toward genuine racial integration and acceptance, Baltimore, like most southern towns, generally lags a few years behind the rest.

Certainly, being the nation's first African-American dean of a majority medical school in 1991 had its pride and glory, both for Wilson and for the school. But not enough to transform the pockets of bigotry and decades of intolerance firmly entrenched in the very institution he was hired to lead. After more than half a century of enduring his share of racism, jealousy, and nay-sayers, Wilson simply considered on-going racial prejudice as an intractable, ever-present irritant in his personal and professional life—irrational and uncontrollable, and, therefore, by definition, not something on which to dwell.

Wilson with Maryland support staff, 1992

Sure, he knew that down here below the Mason-Dixon Line, there were professional and social clubs that would never let him through their private doors. So, what else was new? But what really got under his skin was his own institution. The University of Maryland School of Medicine, a publicly supported school whose founding fathers had made or at least the stated commitment to equality and social justice, welcomed only a sprinkling of African-American faculty and students over the years. Even in 1991, in a city that was predominantly non-white, minorities accounted for only about 8% of the medical school's student body and only 3% of the faculty. Here, on the threshold of the 21st century, Maryland's own home-grown medical school remained a mostly white bastion in the midst of its darker-skinned, inner-city community, including most of the patients treated at the University hospital.

While most people were pleased about Wilson's appointment, not everyone at the school was entirely thrilled to wake up one morning to find a black man—no matter how well credentialed—suddenly at the helm. Some simply responded coolly when introduced; others privately questioned whether an African-American could ever successfully lead a mostly white school.

In the end, Wilson knew his accomplishments at the School of Medicine would have nothing to do with race, but he also knew that in this new, high-profile position he could do more than most people in academic medicine to serve as a role model and door-opener for qualified, under-represented minorities. So, along with all the rest of his ambitious goals, upgrading the school's racial mix to reflect the diversity of the rest of the country was also on Wilson's enormously ambitious to-do list.

But for now, all that would have to wait. Today, on his first day as the new dean of the University of Maryland School of Medicine, in his new office on the 14th floor, in this strange new city, Wilson had more immediate problems to tackle, like getting through more than *five feet* of unopened mail.

Getting Started

Apparently, hundreds of pieces of written correspondence had accumulated since his appointment was announced last spring, most of it irrelevant. There was someone hoping to get their friend into the school, someone looking for information on a rare disease, someone complaining about the hospital. Wilson had to laugh at that one. "As if I had any say over the hospital!"

Later he realized he would have been better off just tossing the entire five-foot tower of mail into the circular file, but in those early days, Wilson plowed through all of it, answering what he thought he had to, and making lists of things to do and people to see. The backlog of paper, along with dozens of people pressing hard for appointments to grab the ear of the new dean, kept Wilson plenty busy for his first several weeks.

> *When you become dean, the first ten or twenty people who want to see you, you can be pretty sure you don't want to see—not now and not ever again. These people are not there to help you. These are the eager beavers only interested in presenting their own agendas and gripes. Many turn out to be the "bad actors," the ones you'd be better off without.*

Coming in at 7:00 am and working to 10:00 pm daily, Wilson eventually whittled down his paper mountains and made room in his calendar to talk to Tyson Tildon, mayor Schmoke, Maryland delegate "Pete" Rawlings, Eli Saunders, and all the department chairs, so he could more fully assess what he had gotten himself into and begin to formulate how to move the school beyond the status quo.

From the start, Wilson knew the school needed three things: A Plan, money to fund the Plan, and a team of dedicated people to help put the Plan into action.

First and foremost, he needed the people.

Early on, Carole Boyer, administrative assistant to the campus president, and Jean Hinton, long-time dean's office secretary, provided valuable assistance to Wilson as he oriented himself to the new campus, assembled his support staff, and organized his new office. Boyer also helped Wilson recruit Jeanette Balotin to fill the newly created position of Chief of Staff, in March 1992, to oversee and direct the dean's perennially busy administrative staff.

The first few weeks were especially hectic. In his first month on the job, Wilson made several trips to Annapolis to meet with legislators, participated in a campus leadership retreat, attended national health policy meetings, sat in on conferences about a proposed merger between UMAB and UMBC, and met with dozens of the people of every description. Soon, some people were complaining that the dean was impossible to see.

"If you want to see me," he told one critic, "come in at seven in the morning, or come in after six o'clock at night, but don't expect to see me in the middle of the afternoon, because I'm scheduled up. If you don't get here before nine in the morning and you go home at five, that's *your* problem."

The line to see the dean was long and growing. Alumni wanted to come in and tell him how to run the school. Faculty wanted to come in and complain about department chairs. Department chairs, accustomed to calling the shots, came in repeatedly, trying to cut deals for more space, for people they wanted to recruit, for courses they wanted to change.

They quickly learned that *this* dean didn't make deals. "You want a curriculum change," he told one department chair, "we'll discuss it at the next executive committee meeting. There's a curriculum committee that is supposed to handle that kind of stuff. I'm not going to make the decision. Oh, and by the way, neither are you."

The constant bombardment wasn't all negative. Wilson got plenty of positive feedback, too. Many people were grateful he had come to Maryland and encouraged him to be as daring as he needed to be to take the school where he envisioned it could go.

With the mountain of mail out of the way, the first round of frantic appointments behind him, and his support team pulling together, Wilson turned his attention to his next priority for the school: Money. Lots of it.

Clearly, more funds from the state would not be coming any time soon. In the 1990s, the country was reeling from one of its worst economic periods since the Great Depression. Across the nation, the economic indicators were down, consumer confidence was low, and unemployment rates were climbing.

Closer to home, the Maryland legislature continued to cut funding for the medical school, which over the years had grown overly accustomed to relying too heavily on the state. Wilson's inauguration as dean came on the heels of two budgets cuts, totally more than $1.5 million. Then in fiscal year 1991-1992, the state sliced the school's budget a staggering eight more times in just twelve months, bringing the two year total to more than $4 million. With reductions No. 7 and 8, furloughs were ordered, first for three days, then for five days.

Wilson felt heartsick, but what else could he do? Laying off people was not an effective way to deal with the school's immediate financial problems because employees often had considerable unused vacation time they could cash in, postponing any immediate financial relief for the school. So furloughs were not especially effective for any school. But they were even more impractical for a medical school.

"What exactly are we supposed to do, just close up shop for a few days while their patients laid around and experiments went unattended?" Wilson wondered. He had no choice but to accept the furloughs, but many people, especially the most conscientious ones, simply came to work anyway, without pay.

Clearly, more realistic solutions were desperately needed. To generate future state funds, Wilson knew he had to make himself known to legislators and share his vision for the School of Medicine. And he also knew he had to go beyond the state to pursue more and larger research grants, philanthropy, and money generated by the Practice Plan to carry most of the budget. On the top of his list was the pressing need to increase research grants to the school.

Wilson was astonished to discover that many Maryland faculty members simply declined to apply for grants if they thought someone from

Johns Hopkins might be competing for the same funding. Apparently, many faculty had accepted second-class status in the shadow of the world-renowned medical colossus in East Baltimore. That attitude, he vowed, had to change and it had to change quick.

Over the years, researchers at Maryland's medical school had grown accustomed to receiving only about 17% of their funding from grants, with the rest of their salaries supplemented by state money.

"A climate like that will destine you to mediocrity for the rest of your life," Wilson explained to the faculty. "Particularly when state funds were evaporating as quickly as alcohol on the skin. The best faculty at the best institutions, public or private, earn most of their keep: Clinicians generate sizable medical care payments and the researchers win substantial grants from the National Institutes of Health, private foundations, and other sources. Going out and getting the money is an essential part of every faculty member's job description."

In open meetings and private conversations, Wilson urged Maryland researchers to explore every grant possibility. They needed to keep current with NIH's frequently issued requests for proposals and applications. They needed to know where to look for research opportunities in their own fields, as well as keeping an eye on the bigger picture to see what else might be available.

For example, the National Center for Research Resources, an NIH institution, funds construction, renovation, equipment, and similar capital expenses that will be used for multiple research purposes. The grants are large and only the strongest proposals win. No one at Maryland had ever even applied for an NCRR grant. Wilson applied and got rejected on the first application, but used the experience to learn exactly what the peer review panels wanted to see. His second application won a $1.2 million grant for the school to construct new research labs. Each of his subsequent grants was funded, opening the door for Maryland to become a regular NCRR grantee.

In time, by coaxing, convincing, encouraging, and when necessary, insisting, Wilson got his message across to the faculty and a new round of grant proposals started going out.

Maryland's First Strategic Plan

Generating more revenues was essential, but Wilson knew that money alone would not transform the school into the innovative institution he envisioned. For that they needed a detailed plan that could serve as a road map to the future. Boyer, who had written a strategic planning document in her previous position, helped Wilson lay out the early beginnings of the School of Medicine's first Strategic Plan.

When Wilson presented his ideas to key faculty and staff, many were left wide-eyed and even speechless. Greg Handlir, associate dean for resource management for twenty years at the School of Medicine had never seen anyone even consider, never mind actually implement, a Strategic Plan for articulating and achieving long-range goals. Handlir knew this type of mission-based management was usually the purview of successful businesses, not sleepy academic institutions.

"That's when I knew this wasn't going to be your average medical school dean," said Handlir. "I knew Wilson was going to be our first medical school CEO. This guy had a clear, strong vision for the school and he was ready to hit the ground running."

One day early in the planning process, when Wilson was talking informally with faculty about his hopes for the future, someone said, "Okay, dean, just give us your strategic plan."

Wilson quickly replied, "Oh no, it's not going to be MY plan; it's not the dean's plan. It's going to be YOUR plan. You will own it."

Toward this end, Wilson brought together a group of faculty and administrators for a retreat, in June 1992, to identify priorities and lay the groundwork for the Strategic Plan. After the retreat, Wilson and the large planning committee led by Jane Matjasko, chair of the Department of Anesthesiology, worked on a consensus building process that was both top-down and bottom-up. The committee interviewed scores of faculty, students, staff, administrators, alumni, legislators, community physicians, community leaders, and others about their views of the school and their hopes for its future.

It took nearly eighteen months to nail all the specifics in place, but when Wilson heard grumbles about how long it was taking, he retorted, "No one has ever done anything like this at this school before. It can't happen overnight."

When it was finally complete, the school's first Strategic Plan covered a five-year period from 1994–1999, dividing priorities into six areas: Faculty recruitment, development, and retention; Curriculum; Research; Graduate education; Clinical practice; and Outreach.

Within each priority area, the details of the Strategic Plan were hammered out by specific task forces and subcommittees. For example, in the area of faculty development, the school aimed to recruit the highest quality personnel, including women and under-represented minorities, as well as to enhance career development, provide resources to fund start-up projects, and make grant applications more competitive. Other goals included evaluating appointments, promotions, tenure criteria, and assuring salary parity with similar academic institutions.

Similarly, the details were worked out in each priority area, from Research to Outreach. And although the strategic plan was innovative, ambitious, even daring, every goal in every area included detailed and achievable objectives, and the concrete steps necessary to reach them.

The dean led the effort, but he never micro-managed the process or imposed his preconceived views.

Handlir recalls that, "Wilson had an absolutely amazing ability to keep us moving forward toward the big goals, and yet he did not impose himself on us or try to promote any one way of doing things. He respected the process and let us do our thing—as long as we were doing it and making progress. The only thing he would not tolerate was giving up or going backwards. It was all about moving the school forward."

For the first time in its long history, the University of Maryland School of Medicine had a written document that clearly articulated its mission and vision in uncompromising terms, and laid out an ambitious but achievable road map for creating a medical school with "national eminence as an academic institution of excellence," a medical school that would be distinguished by its innovation, its interdisciplinary creativity, outstanding faculty, and excellence in both research and patient care.

Sidestepping the Naysayers

Most people at the school eagerly embraced, or at least politely accepted, the dean's new vision for the school and quickly got on board, or at least got out of the way. But right from the start, a small handful of faculty, department chairs, and administrators resisted, and perhaps even resented, Wilson's efforts to stretch the school beyond the status quo.

Lack of support was bad enough when it came from below, but it wasn't long before it became apparent that Wilson would also face challenges from above, as well, as conflicts began with the then campus president.

In the hierarchy of the University of Maryland system, Wilson, as dean of the medical school, reported to Errol Reese, the president of the University of Maryland at Baltimore, the collection of professional schools in downtown Baltimore. Reese reported to Donald Langenberg, the overall Chancellor of the University of Maryland system, who in turn, answered to the Maryland state Board of Regents.

From Day One, the climate between Wilson and his immediate boss was chilly. Reese, the former dental school dean, made little effort to welcome Wilson to the school and was noticeably frosty at social events. Early on, when the president's wife, who happened to be a real estate agent, offered to help Wilson's family find a home in their exclusive neighborhood, Reese quickly put an end to the discussion.

Such petty foolishness had no effect on Wilson's determination to transform the medical school into a leading institution of research and educational excellence. Setting the pace for an all-out frontal assault, Wilson often worked eighteen hours a day, five days a week, with hectic weekend trips to New York to visit his family. Donald's temporary apartment near the school remained mostly empty, strewn with the unpacked boxes and discarded clothes of a man on a mission. He was too busy to be tidy or lonely.

Passing by the dean's office one day, Reese poked his head in and said "Hey, I hear you're putting in ridiculous hours, working all day and all night."

Wilson just stared at the man.

"You know," Reese said quietly with an artificial smile, "Everybody ought to be able to do anything that needs to be done in forty hours a week, don't you think?"

Yeah right, forty hours a week, Wilson chuckled to himself as the president passed. *Show me a man who works forty hours a week, and I'll show you someone who doesn't have much to do.*

The truth was that Wilson handled more telephone calls before lunch than this campus president got all week. What Wilson needed was a team of people who could help make his vision for the school a reality, not a boss who belittled him for putting in the time it took to make that happen.

Wilson found an immediate ally in Carole Boyer, who at the time was Reese's assistant. A savvy administrator with a PhD in higher education management, Boyer had come to Maryland just one month before Wilson's arrival, and she was quickly surmising that their mutual boss, Reese, had only a limited grasp on how to lead the University campus. Not only that, but it also seemed to her that, perhaps because of his dental school background, the president may have harbored an irrational resentment toward the medical school, whose buildings and budgets dominated the campus, dwarfing the other schools.

Reese liked to refer to the medical school as "the 800-pound gorilla," Boyer would later recall. "In his condescending, fake-smile way, Reese asked me to help Wilson 'get off on the right foot.' But it soon became obvious that he intended nothing of the kind."

Boyer liked Wilson from the start and sensed that his unusual combination of laser-sharp intelligence, cool self-confidence, and superb skills and experience were just what the medical school—and the rest of the campus—needed.

In time, Boyer learned that what the chancellor and board of regents most cared about was having a medical school dean who could get the job done. They understood that the fate of the entire Baltimore campus fell and rose with the medical school. Even the hospital, which had been made a somewhat separate entity, couldn't survive without it. So, despite the official hierarchy, Boyer, along with many others on and off campus, knew that the dean of the medical school was more important and more powerful than the president of the campus.

Wilson figured Reese didn't like that too much, but there wasn't much either man could do about it. Wilson never quite understood the man. He knew Reese had his clashes with the dean of the law school, but he never understand what motivated Reese to be so unsupportive of the medical school, whose successes would only make the whole campus—as well as the campus president—look good. The only thing Wilson knew for sure about the president was that he clearly resented underlings who would not behave in a subservient manor.

The word "subservient," however, was never part of Don Wilson's self-generated job description and he had no intention of adding it now. This made for repeated clashes between the two men, who steered clear of each other whenever possible, but who often found themselves at odds over what was best for the school.

For example, when Baltimore's new baseball stadium, Oriole Park at Camden Yards, opened in April 1992, just a few blocks from the University of Maryland, the president insisted on closing the campus. Opening day of baseball season had always been a big deal in Baltimore, and opening day of a brand new stadium was bound to draw exceptional crowds and terrible traffic. Closing the campus made good sense to Reese, and more importantly, it perhaps offered him an opportunity to do something "presidential."

Wilson, however, was not impressed.

"What are you talking about?" he said flatly to Reese over the phone. "We're taking care of patients here. Am I supposed to tell my physicians to go home? If my investigators don't tend to their experiments, their experiments might fail. I should just tell my researchers to go home? Just forget about years of work and expense? Student's have final exams scheduled for that day. To cancel them would raise havoc with the schedule for the rest of the year. No," said Wilson. "The School of Medicine will stay open."

It did, and Reese was furious about it for months. At one point, Reese felt so threatened by Wilson and by anyone who actively supported him, that he actually forbade his administrative assistant to leave her office without his written consent.

"He actually tried to lock me in," said Boyer, who left Maryland in 1993 to become associate dean at the University of Minnesota school of education. "If I wasn't already planning to leave Baltimore, I would have very happily moved to Wilson's office," Boyer said. "He is simply the most brilliant and boldest leader I have ever met."

Tensions between the medical school dean and the campus president got so bad that, despite the good progress on the Strategic Plan and his other initiatives, there were times when Wilson privately thought, *This is crazy, why am I hitting my head against this wall? Maybe I could accomplish more someplace else.*

In fact, the University of North Carolina at Chapel Hill had begun to express interest in him. Their president seemed cordial enough, and their medical school was much better funded and higher ranked than Maryland's. In his quieter moments, Wilson found himself seriously considering the move.

Ironically, it was Reese, himself, who indirectly convinced Wilson to stay put. In what seemed to be a desperate move by the campus president, Reese made his final mistake.

It happened in the late spring of 1993. Back in 1991, when Wilson came to Maryland, the school's finances were so bad that he agreed to start the job with a temporary cut in pay. Now, two years later, the time had come for the school to make good on its original offer to meet Wilson's previous New York salary.

Rankled by what the campus president characterized as a "pay raise," Reese immediately said No, despite the fact that he had originally agreed to match Wilson's former salary. Unfazed by the president's protests, Greg Handlir routinely submitted a request for a salary increase for Wilson, along with others, with the chancellor's knowledge and agreement, effective July 1, 1993.

Reese was livid when he discovered what had happened. He immediately rescinded Wilson's "pay raise" and complained bitterly to university chancellor Langenberg, demanding that the dean return some of his salary. Langenberg, who by now was familiar with Reese's position regarding the dean, did nothing. Reese then wrote several furious letters and memos of protest to Langenberg, some of which eventually circulated to other campus officials and members of the legislature, and in time were leaked to the press.

"U-Md. Dean Allegedly Raised Own Pay," read the *Washington Post* headline. The story ended with a quote from Wilson saying such conclusions drawn from the letters would be "wrong and grossly unfair."

But "grossly unfair" wasn't even the half of it. As soon as the leaks hit the papers, Wilson knew he would stay at Maryland. Not a man accustomed to retreating under pressure, Wilson not only wanted to stay and fight for himself, he shuddered to think what would happen to the medical school if he left, leaving Reese feeling victorious and no strong leader in the dean's office to protect and promote the future of the medical school.

"They'll rape and pillage the place," Wilson confided to a colleague. "And there will be no one here to stop them."

Chancellor Langenberg quickly denounced the leaks and assured the *Baltimore Sun* that "there was no wrongdoing that might warrant disciplinary action." Wilson's salary increase, he explained, was really not a pay raise, but an effort to make good on the original hiring offer to Wilson, which in fact the president, himself, had made.

Undaunted, Reese then ran to the state attorney general's office and demanded an external investigation. Once again, no wrongdoing was found, neither legal nor ethical. Finally, months later, the dust settled and everyone went back to work. Well, almost everyone. Wilson got to keep his previously agreed salary, the School of Medicine got to keep their rainmaker dean-turned-CEO, and the chancellor got to look for a new campus president.

By September 1993, just two years after Donald Wilson first walked the steamy streets of Baltimore to the school's Bressler Research Building and rode the elevator at dawn to the 14th floor, grants and other revenues to the school were rising dramatically. The Strategic Plan was about to be launched. And Errol Reese was gone.

You've got to ac-cent-chu-ate the positive
Eliminate the negative
Latch onto the affirmative
And don't mess with Mister In-Between
You've got to spread joy up to the maximum
Bring gloom down to the minimum
Have faith, or pandemonium
Liable to walk upon the scene

CHAPTER 7

C-Changes
Transforming the Curriculum and the Culture

For the times they are a-changin'
  "The Times They Are A-Changin'"
  By Bob Dylan

Almost everyone everywhere wants something to be different, yet hardly anyone anywhere wants too much to actually *change*. Change can be very difficult, even scary for some people. And radical change can seem all-out intolerable, especially for those who benefit most from the status quo.

Still, the road from Here to Better drives right through the state of Change, and Don Wilson didn't come all the way down from his comfortable home in Scarsdale, NY, to the steamy streets of Baltimore to sit around and watch the weeds grow. Of course he knew there would be uphill battles, but driven by his vision of institutional greatness, Wilson also knew that the University of Maryland School of Medicine was perfectly capable of making, and eventually even accepting, real change. After all, they hired him, didn't they? And recruiting the nation's first

African American dean for a majority medical school was just the latest in a long list of historical "firsts" for the University of Maryland. In fact, during its nearly two hundred years of educating physicians, the school often took the national lead in initiating many vitally important medical education innovations, including:

- First medical school in the nation to require students to take courses in pathology and anatomical dissection.
- First medical school in the nation to teach the techniques of auscultation and percussion in the physical examination.
- First medical school in the nation to add classes in pharmacy into the medical school curriculum.
- First medical school in the nation to require classes in the basic sciences.
- First medical school in the nation to establish a residency program in Family Medicine, spearheading a national trend to better educate frontline primary care providers and the specialists to which they referred.
- First to open a Shock Trauma Center, pioneering the study and treatment of gravely injured patients during the critical "golden hour," the first sixty minutes following life-threatening trauma.
- First medical school in the nation to offer classes in Preventive Medicine.
- …And the list goes on and on.

But Wilson also knew that in the last decade of the 20th century the medical school's once-sharp edge has substantially dulled. Revenues were low, research breakthroughs were infrequent, and despite some notable high-energy exceptions, the place was generally coasting along on low idle.

Two deeply rooted problems were keeping the school from flourishing, and Wilson had no illusions that yanking either of these weeds from the unproductive garden would come easy. The first problem was the medical school's complex and less than ideal relationship with the campus hospital. For as long as anyone can remember, the medical school and the hospital were at odds. "When I arrived in 1991, the situation was just short of pitched warfare," says Wilson. "In fact, the previous medical school dean and the CEO of the hospital hardly spoke to each other, let alone negotiate or cooperate." Clearly, that would not do.

The other thorny issue that simply had to be dealt with was the medical school's terribly out-dated and increasingly irrelevant teaching curriculum, in which independent department chairs taught whatever they felt like teaching, however they felt like teaching it, regardless of what students actually needed to learn. Wilson knew the school would never become the great institution he envisioned until it found the strength to stand on equal footing with the hospital and found the guts to overhaul its out-dated teaching program.

For decades, both of these issues were considered too hot to touch, not just at Maryland but at other medical schools, as well. Across the country, many medical school deans chose to sidestep curriculum reform until they simply had no choice, and the few brave enough to attempt it rarely survived the highly contentious process. Standing up to the powerful hospital seemed even more unlikely. So it wasn't surprising that few people beyond Wilson's closest supporters thought such changes were even possible, let alone imagined that this new dean could somehow pull it off.

Wilson, on the other hand, was ready to get to work.

I knew, coming in, I would have to make some people pretty unhappy around here. Fortunately, that never bothered me too much.

Taking on the Hospital

It seems as far back as anyone can remember, there has always been a struggle between the needs of the medical school and the needs of the hospital, most likely due to the fact that each entity strives to achieve an entirely different set of goals. All talk of cooperation and shared visions aside, the bottom line for the hospital has always been to keep all its beds filled to maximize profits. That means putting a high priority on big-ticket admissions that generate the most money, such as surgery, organ transplantation, and orthopedics.

The primary focus of the medical school, however, has always been quite different. The medical school is in the business of training future doctors and scientists, most of whom will go on to address the garden-variety needs of their patients, such as OB/GYN, pediatrics, and internal medicine, none of which are especially big moneymakers for the hospital. Learning about organ transplantation and orthopedic surgery occupies only about two weeks of the medical school's four-year curriculum. The rest of the time is devoted to teaching future physicians how to deliver good primary care, understand health and health maintenance, prevent disease, and so forth.

While both institutions are motivated by different basic goals, the medical school has traditionally been more sensitive to the hospital's needs than the hospital has been to the medical school. That's because medical schools always have the need to be involved in some form of clinical care, while most hospitals have little need to be involved in academics. In practical terms, the medical school drew nearly a third of its income from clinical care, while the hospital received no direct income from academics—other than the less tangible public relations benefit of being associated with talented medical school faculty who worked at the hospital.

So the motivation to cooperate has traditionally come from the medical school side of the equation with the hospital playing hardball. For decades, the inherent conflict between the basic goals of the medical school and the bottom-line motivations of the hospital provided continuously fertile ground for all sorts of problems between the two institutions, mostly having to do with time and money. In terms of time, the medical school needed faculty to work in the classroom and the laboratory, and the hospital wanted faculty to put down their books and test tubes, and scrub up at the hospital. In terms of money, the faculty wanted to be paid as much as possible by the medical school; the medical school wanted to be paid as much as possible by the hospital (for the time faculty spent working there); and naturally, the hospital wanted to pay the least possible for the most faculty hours it could get.

In the absence of strong leadership at the medical school, powerful department chairs had became accustomed to cutting their own deals with the hospital, bypassing the dean's office and often bypassing the best interests of the medical school in the process.

> *Over the years, the chairs of the medical school's clinical departments had grown quite used to playing both sides against the middle, making separate deals with both the school and the hospital. The hospital was always asking them to do things that were not academic, and the medical school was always asking them to do things that were academic. So there was always a push-pull on the faculty, which they tried to use to their advantage. They made their deal with the hospital; they made their deal with the medical school. The deal they made with the hospital wasn't necessarily good for the medical school. Meanwhile, the hospital would keep it all very confidential; they wouldn't tell the medical school about the deals they had with our people. This sort of thing always happens in a vacuum of leadership. As the new dean, I had to keep reminding the faculty that they work for the medical school, not the hospital.*

Making matters even more challenging was the fact that the hospital, which chronically was in the red at the end of every year, was spun off from the University as a separate not-for-profit institution in 1983. The new entity's governance required that three members of the University System board of regents, the president of the University, and the dean were to be members of the board of directors, and that medical staff members were required to be faculty of the school of medicine. Thus was created the perfect scenario for détente.

However, the new hospital organization had somehow managed to secure the right to call itself the "University of Maryland Medical System." This naturally gave everyone the impression that the University of Maryland medical school was somehow part of the seemingly broader University of Maryland Medical System, which was entirely false. This one small misconception gave Wilson no end of trouble.

> *The University of Maryland School of Medicine is not part of the hospital, nor is the hospital part of us. Unfortunately, the hospital—which is not our hospital—has the name "University of Maryland," and so everybody assumes that it's part of the University, which it is not. They assume that the doctors work for the hospital, which they do not. The hospital can say and do whatever it likes to say and do, and people simply assume it is the University of Maryland saying and doing these things, which it is not.*
>
> *The fact is, all the physicians in the hospital work for the medical school, not the hospital. The medical school hires and fires these physicians, not the hospital. And the medical school pays their salaries, not the hospital.*
>
> *Nevertheless, I had some faculty who, even after years of employment, still did not know they worked for the medical school. Every year, I got a least one request to promote a faculty member who listed on his or her CV that they held a faculty position with the University of Maryland Medical System (the hospital), which in fact was not their employer and which makes no*

> *academic appointments. I usually dropped these CV's directly into the wastebasket. If the person didn't even know for whom they worked, they certainly were not ready to be promoted.*

For services rendered, the hospital does pay part of some medical school faculty salaries, as specified by contract with the medical school, to compensate the school for time faculty spend supervising hospital residents, serving on hospital committees, and providing other direct service that directly benefits the hospital. Their contribution today to the salaries of clinical medical school faculty is on average less than 15%. "It still needs improvement," says Wilson. "However, this support has increased more than fifteen-fold since I arrived. Meanwhile, the hospital gets most of the public relations credit for whatever wonderful clinical work the medical school faculty does on their behalf."

When Wilson arrived in 1991, the historically poor relationship between the medical school and the hospital had deteriorated to virtually all-out war, with an unofficial "I'm not talking to him if he's not talking to me" communications blackout between the top leaders of the two institutions. The first thing Wilson needed to do to begin improving relations was to begin to elevate, in people's minds, the medical school's standing with the hospital. The fact was the two entities were already on equal footing. The challenge would be to convey this reality to his faculty, department chairs, and the then-hospital CEO, Morton Rapoport, MD.

Early in Wilson's deanship, Rapoport joked that word on the street was that the new dean intended to "take back the medical school," meaning Wilson was on the warpath to make sure that his department chairs and faculty knew they worked for the school, not the hospital.

"Really?" responded Wilson. "I wasn't aware that I had to 'take back' anything. They all do work for me already, don't they?" Getting that reality clear in everyone's mind, however, would be an uphill battle over the years. Fortunately, Rapoport and Wilson developed a contentious but personally warm relationship.

Reinventing the Curriculum

At the same time that its relations with the hospital were less than ideal, the medical school had another deeply entrenched problem that Wilson was determined to change: The school's curriculum had grown terribly outdated and increasingly irrelevant.

Back in the 1800s, adding new classes in the basic sciences to the clinical medical curriculum was forward-thinking and bold. The move helped produce a new breed of 20th century physicians who knew enough fundamental science to make some sense of the explosion of new discoveries in biology and biochemistry. But over the years, as various courses were added and deleted based on whatever individual faculty and department chairs felt like teaching, Maryland's four-year program began to grow cumbersome and disjointed. On the threshold of the new millennium, the curriculum was sorely out of date and stalled in the past.

At the heart of the problem was a lack of integration between the basic sciences and the practical activities of becoming a physician, such as learning to make accurate diagnosis and provide appropriate clinical care. For the first two years, Maryland's medical students took lots of science classes, like anatomy, biochemistry, physiology, biophysics, neurosciences, genetics, biostatistics, microbiology, pathology, pharmacology, psychopathology, epidemiology, and others, with little opportunity to see how any of it directly impacted real patients. Instead, faculty and their stand-ins (graduate students and post-doctoral junior faculty) droned on for hours about their narrow research interests to small handfuls of yawning students, who had mastered the fine art of looking alert while taking a mental nap. The rest of the class simply didn't show up.

"After the first few weeks of the new school year, students would stay home in droves," recalled Frank Calia, MD, who at the time Wilson arrived, was vice chair of the Department of Medicine at Maryland.

"Our medical students had eight hours of largely irrelevant lectures and outdated laboratory exercises by day, and then they went home and had to try to teach themselves what they actually needed to learn to pass their tests. If they had a quiz in physiology coming up, they'd skip biochemistry so they could stay home and study. If next week, they had a biochemistry quiz, they would blow off physiology. It was the craziest, most disjointed form of learning you could imagine. It was all about passing the tests and getting through their basic science courses. For the first two years of medical school, students had very little access to the human beings we call patients."

All clinical rotations, electives, and most of their hands-on, practical learning was crammed into the last two years. This was not the most effective way to train the average medical school student, who is usually a sheltered twenty-one-year-old with very little real-world experience. Most medical students are still in their adolescence, often still financially dependent on their parents, their spouses, or the bank. They not only need to learn how to be effective doctors, they often also need to learn how to set up an effective medical practice and manage the complex business side of their profession. More importantly, young would-be-doctors need to learn how to relate to people unlike themselves, and to stay abreast of important new developments in their fields.

But despite the efforts of Calia and others to drag the school's old and disjointed curriculum into the present, every attempt at persuading the department chairs to significantly change the curriculum—the faculty retreats, the endless meetings, the countless memos—all led nowhere.

"It didn't matter what we did," Calia said. "The bottom-line was they just wouldn't budge. For years, committees were formed, meetings were held, but it was just Mission Impossible. The departments felt they owned their courses and they jealously guarded their existence. They were in the habit of using these classes to negotiate with the (former) dean. They would say, 'We have X number of contact hours so we need Y number of faculty and Z number of dollars. Basically, they used their classes to buy leverage for their departments."

That is, until the fall of 1991. Leverage, they were about to discover, was no longer for sale.

Drawing a Line in the Sand

Wilson knew that if the school was to thrive in the coming new century, their medical education program had to radically change. And there was one other pressing reason that the curriculum had to be fixed as soon as possible: They had no choice. The accrediting body of the nation's medical colleges, the Liaison Committee on Medical Education (LCME), which awards accreditation to all the nation's qualifying medical schools, had a very clear message for the University of Maryland: Fix your curriculum!

Every seven years, the LCME conducts rigorous reviews of most medical schools, offering praise when praise is due, making suggestions for improvements where needed, and providing nearly every medical school in the country with continuous, uninterrupted accreditation. Losing LCME accreditation was quite rare and utterly disastrous for any medical school. It certainly was *not* going to happen on Wilson's watch.

> *My predecessor was a nice guy. Maybe too nice. The prior dean knew the school needed curriculum reform, but he also knew the department chairs would have none of it. They wanted everything to stay as it was, with them calling all the shots. When I discovered just how bad the curriculum had gotten, I drew a line in the sand. For too many years, the LCME had found the curriculum to be lacking, and our own internal studies had found the curriculum to be lacking, and now that would have to change.*

For any school, an LCME review is a *very* big deal. It ties up campus resources for months as faculty and staff members prepare reams of written documentation about every aspect of the school as they brace for onsite reviews.

"It's a huge process," Calia said. "A year before they come, they send you a package the size of a New York City telephone book with questions and queries concerning your curriculum, data gathering, your institutional strengths and weaknesses. Then we have umpteen different committee meetings, collecting and studying all sorts of data, analyzing this and that. The whole ordeal is a very arduous, very exhausting.

"Next, they send out a team of about six or seven people, mostly deans or associate deans from other schools and a medical student, to look at your curriculum, your relationship with the teaching hospital, the size of your faculty, the CVs of your faculty, your research productivity—all of it. For four days, they meet with just about every stakeholder in the school: the dean, the students, residents, faculty, everyone. In the end, it's a valuable process, but it's a royal pain in the rear."

As early as 1984, the LCME had reviewed the School of Medicine and found too many lectures, not enough clinical experience, and too little integration between the basic sciences in the first two years and the clinical rotations in the third and forth. The school's basic science courses were called esoteric, uncoordinated, and abstruse. Anatomy, for example, didn't know what physiology was teaching. Biochemistry hadn't a clue what pharmacy was up to, and so on. It was really quite a mess. Three years later, when they returned in 1987, they found little reform.

"Before Dr. Wilson got here," recalled Greg Handlir, associate dean of Resource Management. "There was the occasional talk about curriculum reform. There were plans. There were committees. There was a bit of tinkering, here and there, but nothing ever really changed."

With the arrival of a new dean in 1991, the LCME agreed to give the school a little more time. But not much. If Wilson wanted to save the school's accreditation, he had better do it fast.

Donald called the faculty together in the medical school teaching facility atrium during his first week on the job. "Teaching is the major effort this school needs to put forth," he explained. "One of the first things we have to do is to change the curriculum. It's a very old-fashioned and traditional curriculum. And, by the way, you have a mandate from the LCME to change the curriculum, so it's not as if you have any choice in the matter."

The room went unusually quiet. Calia, who had known Wilson from back in the days when both men went to Harvard and Tufts, was elated. "Wow," he thought. "Let's see if Don can really pull this off." Waiting to shake the new dean's hand after the firm speech, Calia recalled that Wilson had been the first person in their Tufts class to get tenure, the first person in their class to become a full professor, the first division chief, the first department chair, and now the first Maryland dean in a long, long time willing to take on the faculty. "I remember thinking to myself, if anyone can pull this off, it would be Don Wilson," Calia said. "But to be honest, I really didn't think it was possible."

A member of the school's faculty since 1969, Frank Calia knew the place all too well. In fact, by 1991, Calia was fed up with all the roadblocks and looking for a way out. As chairman of the perpetually stymied Curriculum Committee since 1988, Calia was finished being frustrated and was finalizing the details to take over as vice dean at another school.

"Don, I'm probably going to leave," Calia confided in Wilson a few months after his arrival. "I've been hired to turn the curriculum around at another institution, and I think I'm going to run with it."

"That's not such a great place," replied Wilson. "Why don't you just stay here as vice dean and turn *this* curriculum around?"

"That sounds like a job offer," Calia said, surprised.

"It is," Wilson answered.

"Okay, what's my job description?"

"Write it yourself," Wilson said, "then let me take a look at it."

A few days later, Calia handed Wilson his suggested job description, Wilson made a few changes, and the school's new vice dean and senior associate dean for academic affairs moved upstairs to the 14th floor.

"For the first time, I felt we had a fighting chance of making some real changes," Calia said. "We desperately needed to make the curriculum more clinically relevant and we needed to integrate the information across department lines so when a student was learning a biochemical pathway they knew why it was clinically germane. The basic science departments could no longer own these courses; they needed to belong to the school, the faculty, and the students. They needed to be taught, not in separate worlds of their own, but as part of an integrated block."

Blasting Through Faculty Resistance

Calia knew the trick would be to get the faculty, especially the most oppositional department chairs, to go along with it and work as a team. For years, they simply were never held accountable for ignoring directives from the dean's office. Not that the former deans didn't try. In March 1989, dean John Dennis organized a curriculum reform retreat to Easton, Maryland, where he and members of the faculty attempted to create a master plan. Ideas were generated, goals were set, action plans were made, and reams of papers came out of the three-day meeting. It was a valiant effort—except for one problem: Some of the most powerful department chairs never even showed up. "The department chairs really stuck their finger in his eye by not coming to the retreat," Calia said. "Years passed and the old curriculum prevailed."

Now all that would have to change.

Wilson made his position crystal clear to the faculty: The curriculum would be reformed. Period. "It is not a matter of If, because we are going to change it and we are going to do so in a deliberate way. And it is also not a matter of When. I expect a final report on my desk within one year, and I expect to begin implementing our new curriculum by the fall of 1994. This is an essential part of our Strategic Plan. It is not negotiable. Anyone who cannot live with that is free to go."

Some faculty members were upset, some more vocally than others. Many more may have been quietly anxious about how the changes would impact their corners of their departments. Others were genuinely enthusiastic from the start. And a few were hopping mad, particularly the powerful chairs of the basic science departments who, over many years, had grown accustomed to calling the shots.

"It took real guts," recalled Greg Handlir, "for Wilson to say 'enough.' It took real leadership to be able to say to oneself, 'I know I'm going to get a lot of crap for this, I know I'm going to get fierce resistance, but I'm going to do this anyway because it's the right thing to do, because it's in the best interest of our teaching program, because it will save our school.' Believe me, there are lots of deans out there who would never have had the nerve to pull it off."

Wilson gave his new vice dean free reign to explore how best to proceed. Energized by the prospect of real reform, Calia decided to study what other schools were doing to reinvent their antiquated curricula, what philosophies could be applied, what specific steps could be taken. At the time, Harvard Medical School was at the forefront of curriculum reform, as was McMaster Medical School in Hamilton, Ontario.

First, Calia signed up for a curriculum reform course in the fall of 1992 at Harvard. He took a group of Maryland's department chairs with him, making sure he included some who were in favor of changing the curriculum and some who were against it. "At Harvard, we had some dramatic conversions, but others dug in their feet. The ones who were really recalcitrant, simply refused to go at all."

The Harvard trip provided Calia with a blueprint for initiating change and it gave the group its first and most basic tenet: A medical school's curriculum belongs to the faculty and the students, not to the department chairs. *Radical concept!* he thought.

Next, Calia arranged for a group from Canada's McMaster Medical School to come to Baltimore. McMaster was a pioneer since the 1960s in conceptualizing and implementing "problem-based learning" for medical schools, in which students are presented with a problem and have to figure out what they need to know to solve that problem, and then solve it. The program featured small cooperative groups of students engaged in self-directed, self-assessed, problem-based learning—a dramatic shift from the large lecture classes that had characterized much of Maryland's medical education for so many years. While the use of case studies had always been part of the curriculum at Maryland, even in large lecture classes, the idea of creating small discussion groups engaged in self-directed, problem-based learning was entirely new.

To get the reform ball rolling, Calia and his supporters formed a "radically open" Oversight Committee. "Basically, if you were a faculty member or a medical student and you wanted to be on the committee or a subcommittee, you were on it." Headed by Calia, the Oversight Committee also required the participation of *all* department chairs—like it or not, because like it or not, things were going to change.

After months of wrestling with many ideas, the Oversight Committee articulated five main targets for curriculum reform, including problem-based, self-directed, computer-assisted learning, interdisciplinary teaching, greater opportunities for clinical experiences, and more focus on disease prevention. In time, seven subcommittees were formed, each charged with examining a different aspect of reshaping and implementing a new curriculum, including basic science, clinical science, ambulatory care education, faculty rewards, faculty development, informatics, and student evaluation. From these general targets, dozens of specific goals and objectives were identified. It was a huge undertaking, spanning nearly six years. They started in the fall of 1992, launched the new curriculum in 1994, and graduated their first class in the spring of 1998.

Support from the Top

Throughout the entire grueling process of transforming the curriculum, the dean supported those sweating it out in the trenches, while keeping their detractors from blowing the whole thing up.

"Everyone had their say, but Wilson made sure that when people were playing games and being passive-aggressive it didn't stop the process," Calia said. "He met with the students, he met with the faculty, and he listened to people whine and complain and insist on this, that, and the other thing, for hours on end. And he listened to me a lot, too. He became my psychotherapist."

Wilson meeting with student class officers to discuss new curriculum, 1994

With the fiercest opponents to curriculum reform sitting right there on the Oversight Committee, Calia had his hands full. "I have to say, chairing that thing was an experience and a half. Very unpleasant. And bringing the new curriculum to the faculty wasn't exactly a bowl of cherries, either. They said 'Calia, it won't work. The reason it won't work is because we're too busy doing research, or seeing patients, or working in the OR. You will schedule us for a lecture or for one of these small group discussions, and we won't be able to come. Besides, you're not paying us to do this.'

"'Wrong!'" said Calia. "'The portion of their salary that comes from the state is for teaching.' They had to face the fact that if the dean said you're doing it, that means you're doing it."

As part of the changes, the new program now included one afternoon a week in the students' third year in which he or she would go to a clinic and see a panel of patients that the student would follow for a whole year.

"Man, did that cost us a pound of flesh. The intent was for students to have a continuity experience, but when we proposed it, the surgeons were furious. They said 'What? It's Thursday afternoon and my student is scrubbed and in the OR, and now they have to break scrub and go see their patients in the office?'

"Yes, they do," explained Calia.

At one point, things got so bad that several livid department chairs, four from basic science departments and the chair of surgery (who is no longer at the school), marched themselves into Wilson's office and demanded that the dean "immediately fire" Frank Calia. The group bitterly complained that the vice dean was running amok, taking this curriculum reform thing way too far. These changes he kept talking about were crazy. It would never work, the whole thing was completely untenable and unacceptable, and they wanted Calia gone. *Now.*

Unfazed, Wilson let the five men have their say, without responding. When the room finally fell silent, like a drained hot air balloon, the five feet, ten inch dean slowly rose from behind his large desk. "He's doing exactly what I want him to do," Wilson said calmly as he walked the stunned group to the door.

"That was heroic," Calia recalled. "I'm telling you, *nobody* could intimidate this guy."

Meanwhile, Back at the Hospital...

All the while, as the school struggled to reform its curriculum, Wilson also began a concerted effort to improve their chronically adversarial relationship with the hospital. He knew that, like conjoined twins with separate personalities, both the medical school and the hospital depended on each other for their survival and growth, while each had an entirely different set of daily demand, community expectations, and long-range goals. Continuing to feud, however justified or potentially satisfying, would do little good for either institution. And waiting for someone else to step in and solve the problem was pure fantasy. If things were to improve, Wilson knew he would be the one who had to make it happen.

The dean made it plain that the University was going to control all faculty appointments, not the hospital influencing the department chairs to hire people without thinking about their obligation to the school. And the new faculty appointments would have to eventually pull their weight, bringing in research dollars.

> *Whenever a department chair wanted to recruit somebody, I made it a habit to say No, there's no room. And even if there was room, I just said No. If they had X number of dollars available to recruit someone, I told them they could recruit three people with that money, not one. And they had to bring research dollars with them, otherwise they could only recruit one, someone who could develop as a researcher after a couple of years and earn more of their salary. That's one the reasons our research funding went up. People found out if they wanted their salaries to grow, they had to apply for research grants. No more secret deals with the hospital. The hospital paid the school, the school paid the physicians. If the physicians wanted more money, they had to pull in more research grants. Nobody comes to you and says, you know, "I've got ten million dollars here, how about I*

just give it to you." You've got to put in proposals. You have to put in competitive proposals and win.

Although not initially popular, the duel approach of standing up to the hospital while also insisting that faculty do more to bring in research dollars turned out to be a winning combination for the school on many fronts. Everyone had to be part of the school's clinical practice community and everyone was encouraged to apply for research grants. Income from both the Practice Plan and research funding went up significantly. The school's Board of Visitors backed Wilson's CEO leadership style to the hilt, and in time, the faculty reluctantly adjusted and the hospital began to deal more openly and respectfully with the medical school.

Then, in 2003 there was a change of leadership at the medical system that actually further solidified the already improved relationship between the two institutions. When Edmond F. Notebaert became the new president and CEO of the University of Maryland Medical System (the non-profit hospital that is not part of the University of Maryland, despite its shared name), he arrived with the dubious reputation of being a "dean slayer," based upon his previous interactions at the University of Pennsylvania medical school when Notebaert was President and CEO of Children's Hospital of Philadelphia. However, Wilson welcomed the challenge of working with this high energy CEO and in fact had supported his appointment as a member of the search committee.

Notebaert said "As soon as I arrived, we immediately connected, both professionally and personally. We quickly forged a great friendship, as well as a mutually beneficial professional relationship, which has lead to outstanding growth both for the School of Medicine and the University of Maryland Medical System. I have a great deal of fondness for Wilson, personally, and a tremendous amount of respect and admiration for him professionally. I applaud him for taking the School of Medicine to the next level. Dr. Wilson's continued leadership and support of both the medical school and the University of Maryland Medical System has been greatly appreciated."

New Faculty Rewards

As tough as Wilson was while reforming the curriculum and ending secret faculty deals with the hospital, the dean was also sensitive to the faculty's needs. Wilson and Calia both knew it was important that every member of the faculty feel they had a stake in all the changes, and that they could benefit directly from their additional workload.

"We were asking them to do more clinical care. We were asking them to apply for more grants and to do more research. And now we were asking them to do more teaching, and to do it in an entirely different way," Calia said. "We had to find new and creative ways to reward the faculty because they were going to have to work a whole lot harder. Each time we came up with recommendations for faculty rewards, Wilson made sure those rewards were put in place."

The appointment, promotion, and tenure of faculty became especially hot topics as the playing field shifted. Of these, the issue of tenure became the most contentious. The dean's office had come to the conclusion that continuing to link tenure and promotion had become financially irresponsible for the school. The faculty, on the other hand, wanted to keep tenure linked to promotion in order to secure their jobs and income.

The original purpose of tenure was to nurture academic freedom by protecting people who said controversial things from being fired by people who might not agree with their position. Instead, tenure had become a golden ring faculty pursued in order to secure high paying positions, sometimes long after their productivity had declined.

"People would get tenure because of a scientific discovery," says Calia, "then they'd lose their muse and stick around forever, continuing to draw their pay. The school was loosing money on the deal and we couldn't afford to let it continue. We needed to define what tenure was worth in real dollars and separate it from promotion so that one did not automatically guarantee the other."

At first, all this didn't go over too well with the faculty, but Wilson had no choice.

> *My only other option was to get rid of tenure altogether. Since the early 1980s, the medical school had more people tenured than it could afford to pay, but like so many of their problems, the school did nothing about it—even though it was directed to do so by the chancellor. When I arrived, again like so many of the problems, I inherited a difficult situation that had to be addressed.*

The new Appointment, Promotion, and Tenure (APT) policy, implemented in the fall of 1998, separated tenure from promotion, and extended the time period in which to qualify for tenure from 6-7 years to 9-10 years, which was particularly helpful to women raising families. It also recognized and promoted faculty not only for research, but also for their efforts in the classroom and the treatment room.

"After years of neglect, we needed to reward people for outstanding teaching and clinical care," Calia said. "This was not going to come cheap. It was going to cost money, lots of money. Somehow, Wilson made sure he found the resources to pull it off."

Wilson also managed to find the resources to pull off a vital change for the students, as well. While it all seems so terribly routine today, there once was a time, not all that long ago, when the idea of medical students having access to personal computers in the classroom was barely a fantasy. Every day, new discoveries, changing pharmaceuticals, more accurate diagnostic tests, innovative treatments, and continuous changes in nearly every aspect of medicine demanded that the modern physician have rapid access to relevant information. Even as computers were revolutionizing classroom and independent learning in nearly every field in the early 1990s, not a single U.S. medical school required its students to have and use computers. Now, thanks to their new dean and vice dean, every University of Maryland medical student would have their own IBM ThinkPad laptop computer for use in and out of the classroom. Students could plug their laptops into the computer lab to download their course syllabi, assignments, and slides. Today, computers in elementary school classrooms are common. In medical school in 1994, this was nothing short of revolutionary.

For the first time, University of Maryland School of Medicine students had a truly revolutionized curriculum that included self-directed, problem-based learning, using the latest information technology and problem-solving databases. The school formed new alliances with other professional schools on campus, such as nursing and pharmacy. For example, faculty members from the schools of medicine and nursing began to co-teach a class on physical diagnosis in the School of Nursing simulated patient laboratory, while videotaping the students as they took medical histories, performed physical examinations, and made diagnosis.

At the core of Maryland's curriculum change was the fundamental philosophy that each student—not the faculty nor the departments—was in the driver's seat of his or her own medical education, not just during their four years in medical school, but throughout their entire professional lifetimes.

A New Kind of Student

Before long, word was on the street that Maryland had a new, experimental curriculum. "I would submit we started getting a very different kind of medical student," Calia said. "We started getting students who were risk takers, who were comfortable with learning independently. If all you want to do is fill the class with students who will get high board scores, all you have to do is only take applicants with high MCAT scores. But if you want a diverse student body that's interesting, you're going to accept a variety of kids. Sometimes the ones who struggle a bit make the best, most motivated doctors."

The class of 1998 would be the guinea pigs, the first to experience the new curriculum, beginning in 1994. "I loved that first class," Calia said. "The class president, Otha Myles, was a real prince. When some of the students complained about being the first ones to go down the bumpy new road, he'd tell them to stop and remember they were part of something new, something great. He really pulled the class together and helped them feel proud."

A bit older than most of his classmates, Otha Myles had worked for four years as a physician's assistant (PA) at Baltimore's University Hospital before beginning medical school in 1994. Myles, an African American and a Howard University graduate, found the interview process at Maryland to be "a very positive experience."

"The campus seemed to be a nice mixture of friendly people," Myles said. And it didn't hurt that he and his wife and new baby lived in nearby Columbia, Maryland.

But the biggest draw was Wilson himself. "I picked Maryland because I kept hearing about this new dean who was really shaking things up and kicking some butt. I knew going in that the curriculum was radically changing and my class would be the first to ride the wave. That appealed to me."

But Myles didn't fully understand what he had gotten himself into until classes started that fall. "Within two weeks, I gave up all hope that I could continue working as a PA in the evenings. Medical school was going to be more than a full-time job." In his first year, Myles became the student representative on the curriculum committee, and he served as president of his class for the next three years. That put Myles in the unique position of experiencing the curriculum first-hand as a student, as well as witnessing how the dean, faculty, and others responded to student complaints, suggestions, and problems.

"Early on, there were some faculty members who simply didn't like the new curriculum and they let us know about it. And there were students who were wondering why they didn't have the same program as their friends in other medical schools. Why, for example, was there only eight weeks of anatomy? Would that be enough time to learn what we needed to know? Would we be able to pass our boards? There were faculty members who took too long to present their lectures in the allotted time. There were faculty who failed to submit their portions of the class syllabus in time for duplication and distribution to the students before lectures. We had quizzes scheduled too close together and major exams scheduled too far apart. Lots of fine tuning that had to be done, and there was a fair amount of general anxiety among the students, which I tried to allay."

Students were particularly worried about whether they would learn enough to pass their first set of boards, a three-part test called the U.S. Medical Licensing Exam, with the first test given at the end of the second year of medical school.

"Here we were, getting two hours of lecture and two hours of problem-based learning in which they brought us a case from the hospital. We were getting clinical experience in the first year. In the past, all you did in the first two years was take science classes, the kind of stuff you see on the exam. We were the guinea pigs. We were a group of people who had always gotten A's, always expected A's. Now we didn't know what to expect."

Myles found a true ally in Wilson. "The dean was incredibly supportive and helpful, almost fatherly to our entire class. He met with us monthly to ask about our concerns. And whatever it was, the man was on it.

"For example, we had an 'old-school' professor who kept giving us his old lectures that were way too long, running over the class period and ruining our schedules. We brought it to Dean Wilson's attention, and next thing we knew, that professor was no longer on the lecture schedule. Only a dean can do that. He also made every department put their brightest, best, most interactive people in front of the class.

Teaching may not have been their top priority, but Dean Wilson took charge and made it happen."

When Wilson discovered that some students where having financial trouble, he asked the Alumni Association to set up a student emergency fund and low-interest loans.

"The dean was very student-oriented," Myles recalled. "He didn't micromanage, but he got the ball rolling and made things happen. He was clearly interested in how we were progressing as a group and as individuals. He showed real interest in us and our daily lives, in things you wouldn't think a dean would be concerned about."

Despite the early challenges, Myles and his class were thrilled with the extra time for independent study, the reduced lectures, the correlation of basic science with clinical care time, and the many other benefits of the new curriculum. Students were able to study more during the day and get a whole lot more sleep at night.

"That left us more rested and more motivated to interact with faculty in lectures and small discussion groups than the class ahead of us, who still had the old curriculum. Professors were often surprised by our good attendance and the quality of our questions and input. I loved it. I'd be sitting in class with light bulbs going on, thinking, 'Oh, so *that's* what they meant by so-and-so,' and 'Oh, that's what's going on with the patient.' The integrated approach really brought it all together."

The only other snag came in their third year, when the first "guinea pig" class to go through the new curriculum had to go out into the community to health clinics in Cumberland, on the Eastern Shore, and other areas around the state. At first, many students balked. Some were concerned about their safety, going to places they normally wouldn't go. And many worried they couldn't fit the long trips into their study schedules.

Wilson listened to their concerns, but he was not about to back down. A special meeting was called so the dean could help the class of '98 understand why they were going out into the community and how it would make them better doctors, recalling for the group his own experiences as a young medical student sent off to provide medical care for poor patients in and around Boston in the early 1960s.

"Eventually, everyone calmed down and understood this was something being done *for* us, not to us." Schedules were rearranged and off they went, happily converted to the new and improved medical program at Maryland.

In time, even the faculty came around. In fact, some of those who were initially the most resistant to reform discovered they actually enjoyed the changes. Some of the most feared departments began getting positive feedback on student surveys. And faculty members once considered dreadful lecturers began winning teaching awards.

"It was the damnedest thing I ever saw," Calia said. "All and all, it was one of the most interesting experiences I've ever undergone. And I can assure you, we could never have done any of it without Wilson's leadership and support."

Half way through the new four-year program, Wilson decided to institute yet another curriculum enhancement, this time to bring students a deep sense of professionalism as they pursued their new careers. "The purpose of the White Coat Ceremony," recalled Myles, "was to get you out of the student mode, and into the mindset that you are now responsible for people's lives. We were about to step into the new arena of managing patients and feeling like doctors. Someone is always standing in the background, watching everything you do, but now we were the ones who would be out in front, doing the doctoring."

Nearly two hundred people filled medical school teaching facility auditorium, including 157 students. Next to Wilson's chair sat a big cardboard box filled with 157 new, white physicians' coats.

Several speakers addressed the group, including Myles. "I reminded my fellow students that we were at a great school, that we had come so far and learned a lot, and now in the beginning of our third year, we had a job to do. A job that could actually change people's lives."

Wilson spoke last. "He told us that he was proud of us, proud of our accomplishments. He said that we were about to become medical professionals, that we had to act responsibly, that people would be looking at us, counting on us. He said we were stepping up to something bigger than ourselves, and I could see it right there on everyone's face: We all knew it was true. The emotion in the room was unbelievable. Some people were crying."

Then Donald Wilson—the first black dean of a majority medical school, the man who outlasted the campus president, the leader who stood up to the department chairs and transformed a curriculum that no one thought could change—called forth a single line of 157 silent University of Maryland medical students, and one by one, respectfully placed a crisp, white coat upon their shoulders.

"It was transformative. At that moment, each one of us knew we were no longer mere students. We were part of something much bigger than ourselves, something more meaningful than just our own lives. We were part of the medical profession. We were in it. And we were ready to go out there and do what had to be done."

The LCME Returns

After four years of reform, the first class to ride the wave of Maryland's new curriculum came through with flying colors. Despite the early worries, their board scores turned out to be just fine, and the 1998 graduates were more prepared than most to begin their hospital internships. The following year, the next wave of graduates did even better.

So when the LCME returned in January 2000, in the middle of a winter storm that dumped more than a foot of snow on Baltimore and closed schools, government offices, stores, and restaurants all over the state, the survey team was pleasantly surprised. Calia was especially gratified by the good LCME review.

"After all those years of getting nowhere, we got the job done. In the 1980s and 90s, the LCME had decided that every medical school curriculum had to change, not just ours. It was only a matter of degree. Some medical schools care more about their curriculum than others.

Maryland is especially dedicated to education. We are also a strong research institution. Don really revved up our research engine, improving the recruitment and retention of great faculty. He never looked at it as either-or. His vision was always for *both* a top-notch teaching program *and* a stellar research program. It's the same faculty, after all."

In a letter to campus President David Ramsay in 2000, the LCME praised Wilson for his innovative and successful leadership, well-crafted strategic plan, recruitment of effective new clinical chairs, open accessibility to students, integration of basic and clinical sciences, reduction of lecture hours, and increased small-group learning.

Throughout the whole curriculum reform process, Wilson, like his counterparts at other schools enduring their own curriculum growing pains, had to wear many hats. Recalling the ordeal of reforming the Johns Hopkins medical education a few years after Maryland revolutionized its program, Catherine De Angelis, MD wrote:

> *"Responsibility for the curriculum had always been the realm of the department directors, (leading to) a rather disjointed approach to content design and method of teaching. We needed a coordinated curriculum with an overall theme, little duplication, and no omissions. To accomplish this, it was vital to have a single coordinator based in the dean's office. At various times that role involved being a visionary, mediator, target, coach, or cheerleader."*

Clearly, Wilson was all those things. But there was more to the story. Unlike at Johns Hopkins, Harvard, and many other schools that received very large grants from the Robert Wood Johnson Foundation (RWJF) to reform their curricula, the University of Maryland never got a dime of RWJF support. For some reason, before Wilson arrived, Maryland never applied for a RWJF grant, and by the time he came in 1991, the money was gone, all doled out to other schools. Left out of the curriculum-reform funding fest, Wilson and company would have to pull themselves up by their own blood pressure cuffs.

A few years later, a group from Harvard decided to study the impact of those huge RWJF grants on the quality and effectiveness of curriculum reform, looking at medical schools that had received RWJF money, as well as those that did not. To many people's surprise, the Harvard study found that the University Of Maryland School Of Medicine had one of the most interesting and innovative new curricula they had ever seen—all without one penny of RWJF support.

CHAPTER 8

The Wilson Effect
Think Big, Deliver Bigger

*"You do something to me
That nobody else could do"*
　　　　　　　You Do Something to Me
　　　　　　　By Cole Porter

    No dean, no matter how talented, can get too far without the participation of thousands of people from every nook and cranny of the school. Just how far any dean can take his or her institution is a direct result of the impact the dean has on others, not only to inspire and motivate in good times, but also to command and sustain when the going gets rough. Good deans know they must strive for this; legendary deans do it automatically, like breathing.

    Throughout his fifteen years at the University of Maryland School of Medicine, Wilson's bold vision for the school, his fearless honesty, his relentless work ethic, and his unique CEO-style of leadership have driven him—and more importantly, have driven those around him—to accomplish more than most people thought possible. Wilson's instinctive ability to squeeze more out of people than even they themselves expected has made this powerhouse dean a few enemies and many, many loyal allies and fans.

"Don Wilson loved this school and that love showed, even when it has been tough love," says Pat Madden, who directs the school's Office of Development, another one of dean's many initiatives that became a reality under Wilson's leadership. "There are very few men who can look you in the eye and tell you what they really think. That takes courage. It also makes him a formidable leader and a man very, very hard to say No to."

Many also say this dean is a man you do *not* want to disappoint—not because he will berate you (although, on occasion, he may) but because his expectations have always been so high (for himself and for others) that it is easy to get swept up in the momentum of his goals and end up pushing yourself beyond your own self-imposed limitations.

Call it the Wilson Effect. Simply put, he thinks big until you think big, too. Here's how it works, according to the late Maryland researcher, teacher, and pediatrician Tyson Tilden, MD, who witnessed and participated in many of Wilson's major reforms and projects over the years:

> *At first, it all seems impossible. As a matter of fact, when you first hear about Wilson's plans, you might actually think he's joking because there's simply no way any of it could possibly happen. Then, after a while, you begin to realize this man really means it; he fully intends to do whatever it is you think is so impossible—like build a huge Health Sciences complex, for example, while the state is cutting our funding. And as you listen to him talk, you think to yourself "Come on, man, get real!" You may even need to bite your lip to keep yourself from cursing out loud from the sheer improbability of it all.*
>
> *But then you watch him and you begin to see him make things happen, systematically, one piece of the puzzle at a time, and you think to yourself, "My God, this guy just might pull this*

thing off!" And I'm telling you, somewhere in there it dawns on you that you do NOT want to let this man down. If you told him you would do something—even if it's something you're not entirely sure you can actually do—believe me, you do it. And when you're finally finished with your part of it, you stand back and say to yourself, "Wow, look at what I've done!"

Multiple that by hundreds of people, from faculty to support staff, from students to administrators, and over time the Wilson Effect created a quantum leap of progress for the school. Bold vision and relentlessly high expectations for himself and others have also earned Wilson tremendous respect among his colleagues, such as Jessie Harris, former dean of Maryland's School of Social Work. "Wilson always insisted on excellence," recalls Harris. "He didn't just show up for work everyday and coast; he showed up everyday to get a job done, a big job. And he expected nothing less from those around him."

Being Dean: A Day in the Life

Few people outside the dean's office have any inkling of what the chief academic officer of a medical school actually does, day in and day out. For starters, medical school deans help recruit and retain students, recruit and mentor faculty, and recruit and train post-doctoral students. They also help structure and maintain the clinical practice program, motivate and support research, and plan and engage in endless fund-raising programs and activities. Medical school deans must also meet with alumni, develop relationships with political representatives, address the media, serve on various committees, and offer community service in a variety of ways. Any one of these activities could easily take up enough time to be full-time jobs, even without the near constant "wildcards" that are routinely thrown into the mix, such as surprise visitors, emergency phone calls, and the nearly continuous, unexpected turn of events that result from unanticipated budget cuts, black-outs, or strikes.

At Maryland, Wilson's work day often starts with an early-morning meeting with hospital leadership, Practice Plan Board of Directors, state legislators, or prospective new faculty or staff. Next, he may move on to various in-person or telephone meetings with faculty, the university president, the Dean's Council, student class officers, hospital leadership, department chairs, program directors, staff team meetings, reporters, and various fund-raising activities. In between, he will also attempt to open his mail, read journal articles, review and sign documents, dictate letters, reply to e-mails, and return phone calls.

To all this, add the inevitable last-minute meetings, surprise telephone calls, unexpected visitors, occasional speeches and trips out of town, and various other big and small emergencies that trump previous plans or must be wedged in and around immovable obligations. For example, the campus president may call to say an important committee of the state legislature is on its way (unscheduled) and they simply "must" have an hour with the dean. Or perhaps a potential donor "just happens" to be in town and can only see the dean this afternoon. The classic "wildcard" is a last minute call from someone who simply must see the dean today, "only for a minute." A half hour later, the dean is deeply enmeshed in a complicated issue that will require many additional phone calls and discussions.

Every once in a while, the daily "wildcard" is truly *wild*—like the time when the National Aquarium in Baltimore called to ask dean Wilson, as a physician and liver specialist, to hurry down to their mammal pool to help diagnose and treat a sick dolphin.

> *The physical examination was very interesting, certainly not my typical patient. The Aquarium veterinarians had exhausted all possibilities, and while I knew what should be done, it just was not practical for me to continue to treat the mammal on a daily basis. Luckily, when she died, the newspaper did not mention that I was the consulting physician.*

Wilson's most enjoyable dean duties include welcoming the Freshman on their first day of class, overseeing the White Coat Ceremony to affirm medical student's commitment to professionalism early in their careers, addressing the graduating class at the School of Medicine Convocation, and speaking at faculty and staff award presentations, and at the openings of new buildings. Such pleasantries punctuate Wilson's otherwise grueling work pace, which typically starts at seven o'clock in the morning and often runs late into the evening.

Whatever the day dishes out, the dean's work is not necessarily done when he finally gets home. There, he often reviews additional reports, briefings, and other documents before returning the next day and starting the whole thing all over again.

"The pace is relentless," admits Wilson, "Especially if you want to actually get something done."

Of course, not every dean works this hard. Some simply function as "caretaker deans," maintaining the status quo, meeting and greeting, and attending high-profile campus events. Many other dedicated and talented deans do attempt to make significant institutional changes for the betterment of their schools, sometimes eventually leading to their own demise.

But few, if any, medical school deans have managed as Wilson did to tackle the job like a rain-maker CEO, dragging the outdated status quo kicking and screaming into the 21st century, while the state slashed at the budget, the formidable Johns Hopkins University flexed its muscle across town, and the growing trend toward managed care nipped at the bottom line. Throw in a couple of frivolous lawsuits, a few disgruntled faculty, some rebellious department chairs, the threat of losing accreditation, and 1001 little and big problems from dawn to dusk, and it's a wonder that Wilson didn't quietly retreat into his office late one night, many years ago, and start packing.

"Thank goodness he stayed," says Jeanette Balotin, Wilson's chief of staff since March 1992. "There simply is no way we could have come this far without him."

The Wilson Effect: Maryland in Bloom

Aiming high, often much higher than most people are accustomed to, has been a mainstay of Wilson's unstoppable work ethic at every stage of his professional life, and clearly has been the driving force throughout his deanship at Maryland. Just how very far the University of Maryland School of Medicine has managed to come under Wilson's leadership since 1991, almost defies summation. The school's massive list of breathtaking accomplishments includes hundreds of thousands of square feet of new research and clinical space covering many city blocks, hundreds of millions of dollars in increase revenues to the school, more than a dozen new departments and programs, greater racial diversity among students and faculty, initiation of the school's first Board of Visitors, establishment of the Office of Development and the Office of Public Affairs, an entirely updated and improved medical education curriculum, a complete overhaul of school-wide Information Technology, total revamping of the clinical practice plan leading to the end of annual deficits, and countless new initiatives, policies and procedures that have increased efficiency, funding, and productivity at every level.

More than a dozen years after Wilson took the helm, annual research grants and contracts to the school have not merely increased, they *quadrupled*, propelling the University of Maryland School of Medicine into the top tier of American medical institutions in research funding, despite declining financial support from the state. Ironically, the nation's first public medical school is now ranked dead last in state support among its peers. Few people realize that the state of Maryland provides less than 5% of the school's funds, leaving its medical school to function more like a private institution, such as Johns Hopkins, but without the freedom from state controls and bureaucracies.

Wilson's strategy of treating the medical school's finances like a real-world business, rather than an inefficient government agency, is among his most defining contributions to the University. Under Wilson's direction, the medical school surpassed their Bicentennial goal of $200 million in annual research funding—six years early. During Wilson's deanship, total revenues to the school exploded from $190 million in 1991 to $624 million in 2005, boosting the school from the bottom third to the top fifth of all medical schools in the nation. According to the latest data from AAMC annual reports, Maryland's School of Medicine now ranks eighth among seventy-seven public medical schools in federal research expenditures, fourth in research funding per clinical faculty member in public medical schools, and fifth per clinical faculty member in all medical schools, public and private.

Endowed professorships rose from just two in 1991 to forty in 2006 as the school has grown to twenty-four departments, seven academic programs, and five organized research centers. Wilson personally recruited all but two of current department chairs. With its emerging stature as a leading research and cutting-edge medical education institution, the school rapidly evolved from its former role as the "fall back" school for local kids who couldn't make it into the big leagues, to the new "first-choice" medical school of many highly qualified applicants here and across the nation.

During this time, Maryland's rainmaker dean was also named "The Nation's Dean" as chairman of the Council of Deans of the American Association of Medical Colleges (AAMC), an institution representing all of the nation's allopathic medical schools, over four hundred teaching hospitals, and thousands of faculty members, students and resident physicians.

In 1992 Maryland had three commissions regulating hospitals and health care in the state. When William Richardson, chairman of Maryland's Health Care Access and Cost Commission and president of Johns Hopkins University left to move to Michigan in 1994, the governor called upon Wilson to chair the commission. And when the Maryland General Assembly sought to streamline the state's health-care regulatory system in 1999 by merging two commissions into the new "Maryland Health Care Commission," their respect for Wilson's knowledge and integrity was such that the legislation was written with the mandate that he head this venture as well.

Wilson is a former member of the Emergency Medical Services Commission of Maryland, and holds memberships in many prestigious medical and research societies, including the Institute of Medicine of the National Academy of Sciences, the Association of American Physicians, and the board of directors and vice president of Alpha Omega Alpha, the nation's medical honor society. And if all that isn't enough, dean Wilson is also a Master of the American College of physicians, an honor bestowed on less than 1 percent of its members.

In his "spare" time, Wilson somehow also managed to sit on several boards of local organizations, including the Baltimore Symphony Orchestra, the Baer School, the Kernan Hospital Endowment Fund, Provident Bank, Mercy Medical Center, and the University of Maryland Medical System, among others. His numerous national and local awards include the University System of Maryland's Frederick Douglass Award, the Baltimore Urban League Whitney M. Young, Jr. Humanitarian Award, the Towson University Distinguished Black Marylander Award, and the AAMC's first Herbert W. Nickens Diversity Award for Wilson's tireless efforts to promote justice in medical education and health care.

Meanwhile, back on campus, under the dean's guidance, the school's Faculty Council was renewed and the Executive Committee sprang to life; the first White Coat Ceremony was established to help give students a deeper sense of purpose and professionalism; Strategic Plan I was conceived and fully implemented, immediately followed by Strategic Plan II (also fully implemented); the school's Appointment, Promotion, and Tenure policies were thoroughly overhauled; a Blue Ribbon Task Force on Alternative Funding was established; Mission-based Budgeting was introduced with great success; the school's relationship with its Alumni Association was bolstered; the MD/PhD program was improved ... and the list goes on and on.

Any one item from this huge inventory of accomplishments would have been legacy enough for any medical school dean. Taken together, the Wilson Effect has been nothing short of stunning.

The Wilson Effect

"When you stand back and look at the sum of it, it's almost incomprehensible how far we've come," says Vice Dean Frank Calia, MD.

University System of Maryland Chancellor William "Brit" Kirwan, PhD. agrees. "Dr. Wilson was the right man at the right time for our medical school. His vision led the University of Maryland School of Medicine into the top echelon of American medical schools. That is a legacy only a very privileged few can boast."

No longer dozing in the shadow of Johns Hopkins, the University of Maryland School of Medicine has clearly arrived as a world-class medical institution.

A Lifelong Commitment to Diversity

Throughout his career, from clinician to researcher, division chief, department chair, and dean, Wilson has worked tirelessly to attract and support minorities in academic medicine. As dean, Wilson has been painfully aware of how deeply entrenched racism remains in our culture today, both overtly and subconsciously.

> *The fact is, the only time many white medical school students have interacted with black people is when blacks provide a service, such as cleaning their houses or serving their hamburgers. Professional or social interactions on an equal footing is simply not the norm.*

Meanwhile, 40 percent of our nation's future patients will be African American, Latino and other minorities. "How are we going to appropriately train our students to take care of all of society if they don't have the opportunity to see minorities as peers and in positions of leadership and authority?" wonders Wilson. Persistent disparities in how physicians care for minority patients are heartbreaking—in some cases, quite literally.

> *A doctor today can have two patients, one white and one black. They both can have mild hypertension, but sometimes only the white patient is prescribed medication to lower blood pressure and reduce the risk of heart disease. Why? Because the white doctor thinks black people are supposed to have mild hypertension, so they don't need to be treated. Actually, I've experienced this myself. The general level of ignorance is truly staggering.*

Although it has been a lifelong drive, Wilson's official campaign to boost diversity in academic medicine began in earnest in 1986, when he along with several colleagues founded the Association for Minority Academic Physicians (AAMP) with the hope of attracting and supporting more underrepresented minority physicians and scientists. "He started the organization but he never was its president until 2004," said Tilden. "Instead, he chose to serve as secretary. He's a powerhouse, but he's not the kind of man who likes to rub your face in it."

Over the years, the AAMP has worked to bring more diversity to medicine, offering minority summer research fellowships to ignite interest in research and academic careers among minority youth. As a group, underrepresented minorities, including African American, Native Americans, mainland Puerto Ricans, and Mexican Americans, rank well below the national average in education, employment, and health.

While minorities currently make up about one quarter of the U.S. population, they represent only a tiny fraction of medical and research professionals. During the 1950s and early 1960s, minorities accounted for only about 3.5% of all graduates from U.S. medical schools. More than half of these were African American, most of whom graduated from just two institutions, Howard University and Meharry medical schools. When Wilson graduated from Tufts University medical school in 1962, he was one of only three African Americans, boosting Tufts numbers to more than double the national average for non-minority medical schools at that time. Wilson was the only person of color in his residency training program and he saw no African American faculty during his medical school or residency experiences.

Following the Civil Rights Act of 1964, some medical schools began to address the problem of minority under-representation in medicine. By 1975, the number of minority medical school students rose significantly to more than 8%, then stalled for the next fifteen years and eventually grew again in the early 1990s, topping out at just over 11% in 1994.

More recently, with affirmative action and other programs increasingly under attack, the number of underrepresented minority physicians has begun to fall again, with a dramatic decline in male African American medical students. Currently, 65% of all African American medical school applicants are women.

The statistics for minority medical school faculty are even more discouraging. In 1992, when the minority student numbers were temporarily climbing, underrepresented minority faculty weighed in at only 3.5% of full-time medical school faculty nationwide, with more than one third of these at historically minority medical schools and minority medical centers. By 1999, minority faculty increased to 4.5%, in part because a few schools like the University of Maryland have made an effort to attract minority physicians to academia. But many medical schools today have no minority faculty at all, and when they do, their minority faculty are less likely than white faculty to be promoted, achieve tenure, or receive NIH grants.

"America is often described as a melting pot of people and cultures," says Wilson. "I'd say it's become more of a boiling pot, with assaults against affirmative action and charges of racism running rampant." Wilson says he agrees with Jesse Jackson, who once said, "I keep hearing about the melting pot. All I can say is, we haven't melted."

With fewer minorities applying to medical school at the same time that our nation is rapidly growing more ethnically diverse, Wilson fears the so-called melting pot is headed for a meltdown. By the year 2030, ethnic minorities are expected to account for nearly half the population.

Wilson's Way

It's already happened in California, which became the first nonwhite-majority state in 2000, followed recently by Texas and New Mexico.

> *We haven't seen such a rapidly changing population in this country since the 1800s. To practice good medicine, a physician has to be both medically and culturally competent. We must create an environment where differences are accepted, embraced, and valued. This will enrich our institutions and our nation. We must commit to diversity as a value that is central to the very concept of medical education. I believe that students benefit significantly from an education that takes place within a diverse setting. It is a positive experience to learn from others who have backgrounds and characteristics very different from your own.*
>
> *I believe the face of medicine needs to reflect the face of America. The practice of medicine is, after all, a noble calling. Our profession must remain committed to the highest of American values: fairness, equity, and opportunity.*

It took 144 years after the first African American was allowed to enroll in a U.S. medical school for Donald E. Wilson to become the nation's first African American dean of a majority medical school in 1991. Since Wilson, only four other African Americans have achieved the position. When Wilson took over in Baltimore, there was only one woman dean. Today, over twenty medical schools are led by women.

> *When I entered academic medicine I quickly found out that a very effective affirmative action program was already in effect. It's called the Old Boys Club and its members are white males. But I never allowed that to stand in my way, and I try not to let it stand in the way of those around me.*

As dean, Wilson has remained committed to making medicine, and particularly academic medicine, welcoming to minorities. Under Wilson's watch, Maryland's medical school has boosted the participation of underrepresented minorities and women in every arena, creating one of the most diverse student bodies in the country. In 2003, 19% of the entering class was made up of underrepresented minorities. And in 2005, 61% were women, an all-time high. The school's MD/PhD program boasts a 23% diversity level, which is among the best in the country. The school also exceeds the national average for underrepresented minority faculty (7% versus 3.5%), while the total number of minority faculty has quadrupled since Wilson arrived in 1991. Of these, three serve as department chairs and two are associate deans. Nearly one third of the faculty members are women.

While a few have accused Wilson of reverse discrimination, some even going so far as filing (and losing) lawsuits against him, the dean insists nothing could be further from the truth.

> *We had no quotas. I simply hired the most qualified people for the job, without leaving anyone out simply because of their race or gender. All that is really needed to improve diversity is sensitivity to the need for greater minority and gender participation. People who think I show favoritism are incorrect. The fact is that my presence in a leadership position has provided a milieu conducive to the recruitment and retention of minority students, faculty, and administrators. Basically, they felt welcome, so they applied. They were qualified, so I hired them. It was that simple. Believe me, if they were not qualified, you can rest assured they certainly would not be here. And if they weren't qualified, how have we done so well?*

While Wilson had no mentors to guide him on his way, the dean initiated the Office of Student and Faculty Development, in part to provide mentoring opportunities for every Maryland medical student. Wilson also helped establish a new master's program in Public Health, and was the principal investigator on a $4.3 million NIH grant obtained in 2003 to fund the University of Maryland Center for Health Disparities to greatly expand the school's health disparities research and outreach. Established in 2004, the center promotes equal access to healthcare and attempts to ease existing ethnic, racial, geographic, and socioeconomic differences in diagnosis and treatment. The center specifically targets renal and eye diseases, cancer, and other health problems that are prevalent in the predominantly African American Baltimore community. In 2006 Wilson established the "Program of Minority Health and Health Disparities in Education and Research," the seventh academic program he established.

In addition to his work at the University of Maryland, Wilson has also held several key federal positions, including chairmanship of the National Institute of Health's Digestive Diseases Advisory Board, the food and drug administration's gastrointestinal drugs advisory committee, the Agency for Health Care Policy and Research Advisory Council, and membership on the Advisory Committee to the Director of the NIH. At every opportunity, dean Wilson has tried, and in many instances succeeded in raising awareness about the pressing issues of racial disparities in health care and the vital need for greater diversity in academic medicine.

Recently, former Maryland medical school student Mallory Williams, an African American who graduated in 1999, sent the dean a card in which he wrote:

> *It is with great pride, on this 50th anniversary of Jackie Roosevelt Robinson breaking the "color line" in baseball, that I congratulate you on what has been an amazing display of progressive leadership as the dean of the University of Maryland medical*

school. I was not born to witness the triumphs of Mr. Robinson, but I am truly proud to have had the high honor to witness the deanship of Dr. Donald E. Wilson, the "Jackie Robinson" of American allopathic medical school deans.

Although touched by the alumni's kind words, Wilson can't help but point out that Jackie Robinson was a great baseball player, not a great *black* baseball player. "Must we continue to make this distinction?" laments Wilson. "You can tell we're not there yet when people keep talking about *black leaders*—as if it's some entirely separate category. Ever hear anyone refer to *white leaders?*"

Changing the Culture, Wilson's Way

In a lifetime of crossing—and in many cases tearing down—the color line, Wilson seems most tickled by one quiet little accomplishment that will never appear on his resume.

Since way back in the 1800s, about two dozen "white leaders" from Baltimore's two medical schools have come together six or seven times a years for an exclusive black tie dinner and leadership presentation. Over the years, the exclusive group, which calls itself "The Monthly Reunion," has invited certain deans and top physicians from Johns Hopkins and the University of Maryland medical schools to become members, with half the members coming from each institution. Membership in the private club is by invitation only. Blacks, women, and Jews need not apply. Any member was free to nominate anyone they wished to join, but it only took one naysayer to block a nomination.

Wilson's predecessor, John Dennis, had been a member, as was nearly every Maryland dean before him. But conspicuously, when Don Wilson became dean in 1991, he was not invited to join. Frank Calia, as the school's vice dean (and a white male), was invited. University of Maryland Baltimore campus president David Ramsay, also white, who came to Baltimore several years after Wilson, was also invited (although he refused to join). And, of course, over the years, the white medical school deans from Johns Hopkins University were all invited, along with other Hopkins notables. All white. All men.

Repeatedly, Calia nominated Wilson for membership, and repeatedly his nomination was shot down. Calia and some others at Maryland were angry, but Wilson was hardly surprised. "Baltimore is a Southern town. People talk a good game about diversity, but few people actually mean it." After a while, Calia gave up trying to nominate Wilson, and resigned from the Monthly Reunion.

Then in 2003, the exclusive group decided to finally offer Wilson a seat at their table. Wilson flatly refused to join. After a while, a group of Maryland members came to Wilson and asked him to reconsider joining the club, saying it would be in the best interest of the school to have their dean there. "I don't understand why it is good for the school now for me to join, and it was not good for the school in the past."

No one had an answer for that.

Wilson considered the situation carefully. Rather than come quietly, grateful for the late offer, the dean seized the opportunity to turn the awkward situation to his advantage—Wilson's Way. After joining, Wilson teamed up with the dean of the Hopkins medical school to co-write an open letter to the group, essentially saying "enough is enough." The two leaders insisted that the club drop the old rule that allowed a single member to block a nomination, and replace it with a two-thirds vote to confirm a nomination. It was high time they got used to the fact that medical leaders came in a variety of colors, gender, and religions. This was, after all, the 21st century.

The group agreed in a 20-2 vote. A year later, at a black-tie dinner meeting of the Monthly Reunion, Wilson brought as his guest the chairman of Maryland's ophthalmology department, to introduce as a potential new member. At the next meeting, the members agreed to invite Eve Higginbotham to join the historic club, as their first black female member. Today, Wilson is deeply pleased that the Monthly Reunion now includes two women, an African American, and several Jews.

"Now *that's* how you change culture!"

Wilson and U.S. Surgeon General David Satcher celebrating Wilson's 10th anniversary as dean. Satcher was one of several national speakers at a health symposium honoring Wilson, 2001

Wilson with J. Tyson Tildon, Ph.D. at Wilson's 10th Anniversary celebration

Wilson's Way

Wilson receiving Fredrick Douglass Award from University System of Maryland, Board of Regents, 2002

University of Maryland School of Medicine Accomplishments During Dean Wilson's Tenure

- Revenue increased from $190 million in FY1991 to $624 million in FY2005
- Grants and revenues to the school quadrupled from $71 million in FY91 to $350 million in FY05
- Appointed 23 department chairs
- Created three new departments, six organized research centers and five programs
- Recruited 1,900 new basic and clinical science faculty
- Percent of under-represented minority faculty increased from 3.5 in 1992 to 7.1 in FY05
- Percent of under-represented minority students in first year class increased from 8 to 16.
- 4,700 medical students have graduated
- Outdated curriculum entirely revamped to include interactive learning, holistic treatment, and cutting-edge information technologies
- Nation's first medical school to require laptop computers for students
- State-of-the-art research facilities increased to nearly 500,000 square feet
- According to the latest data from the AAMC annual reports (2005-2006), the School of Medicine ranked 7th among 76 public medical schools in federal research expenditures, and 19th among all medical schools. When looked at in terms of funding per faculty member our clinical faculty ranked 4th in research funding per faculty member in public medical schools, and 6th in all medical schools public and private.

CHAPTER 9

Wilson's Words to the Wise
Seven Suggestions for Deans and Other Leaders

*"The record shows, I took the blows,
And did it my way."*
                From Frank Sinatra's signature
                song "My Way"
                By Revaux, Francois, and Anka

Whether you are a current or aspiring academic dean, or the head of any organization, this much you can count on: It may not be lonely at the top, but you most certainly will be *alone*. No matter how many allies you have in your corner, as the person in charge, the buck ultimately stops with you. It's up to you to set the team's goals and standards, to solve the seemingly unsolvable, and to make the countless decisions that lead others to triumph or failure. Everyday you are in the driver's seat carries enormous responsibilities. Even doing nothing is an active choice with definite consequences for which you and you alone are responsible.

Despite the recent flood of books about lofty leadership ideals and the various habits of highly effective people, here, in the real world, when everything goes to hell, the phones start ringing like mad, and angry people are banging on your door, there are no pithy instruction manuals to consult, no sage gurus to reveal your hidden opportunities. Even when things are going spectacularly well, there is no one to show you what to do next. For better or for worse, in the countless golden moments when real leadership is needed most, it's just you out there, flying by the seat of your pants.

In light of this reality, what can a medical school dean, or anyone for that matter, tell you about how to do your job? In truth, every leader sinks or swims on his or her own merits, skills, and wits. Many of the most essential leadership qualities cannot even be clearly articulated, never mind successfully taught.

Still, wise men and women have always strived to learn from each other, and who better to learn from than a passionately productive, tenaciously successful medical school dean, a man who despite every obstacle has managed to master one of the world's challenging jobs—a relentlessly demanding, highly coveted job that hardly anyone knows anything about.

Even folks vying for the position often don't know what they're getting themselves into. Being dean of a major medical school is an occupation that highly accomplished people work decades to achieve, compete fiercely for relatively few openings, take a while to settle into, and then, in about the time it takes to get an undergraduate degree, the majority of them simply pack up and quit.

Deanship can be so daunting that some school leaders privately joke about the legend of *The Three Envelopes*. As the story goes, an outgoing medical school dean assured his newbie replacement that if things got really bad, he could always unlock a secret drawer in his new desk and find three envelopes that would guide him on his way. Sure enough, soon after the welcoming parties ended, the relentless demands and complaints started rolling in: Not enough money for such-and-such; Too little time for research; How come so-and-so always gets a brand new whatsit every year and I never get one? *Always someone complaining!*

When things got bad enough, the new dean went to his secret desk drawer and retrieved Envelope Number One. Inside, a handwritten note said, "Blame Your Predecessor." Bolstered by this time-tested advice, the new dean felt back on track ... for a while. But in time, the problems reappeared and faculty complaints returned louder than ever, and once again the distraught dean went to his secret drawer and opened Envelope Number Two, which simply said, "Reorganize."

This too proved initially helpful, but soon led to even greater faculty anxiety and unrest, with endless meetings and countless committees failing to drive forward any real institutional reforms.

Finally, late one night after an especially difficult week, the exhausted dean groped through the desk drawer, tore open his last note, and was flooded with relief to read, "Prepare Three Envelopes."

Retelling the story, Wilson likes to add, "Of course, when I looked in my drawer at Maryland, I had only *the first two* envelopes!"

But that doesn't begin to explain how Wilson managed to last *fifteen years* as dean of the University of Maryland School of Medicine, more than a decade longer than the average 4.2-year deanship. At any given time, about twenty-five or so of the 125 medical schools in the United States are hunting for new deans, with search committees considering hundreds of top candidates. Apparently, despite the considerable prestige of the position, job turnover is fairly brisk and longevity is unusual.

No one really knows why job turnover is so high. One small study published more than a decade ago, confirms the general perception that, on average, medical school deans do seem to be moving on to other positions sooner than ever before. Insiders blame the relentless stress that comes with the territory, especially for deans who wish to go beyond a figurehead role and actually get something done.

"It's a tough job for anyone trying to make significant reforms," says Maryland's medical school vice dean Frank Calia, MD. "Traditionally, two things kill a medical school dean. The first is trying to reform the curriculum, which means messing with how faculty members teach.

The second is trying to reform the practice plan, which means messing with how faculty members get paid. The practice plan and the curriculum are often the last remaining fiefdoms of the department chairs. Going after either of these hot potatoes can do you in. Don Wilson took on both of these dragons with great success. The difference is strong leadership. You can't be faint at heart and get too far in this job."

On the subject of job endurance, Wilson likes to quote a neighbor who once told him, "A scared man can't gamble and a jealous man can't love," meaning if you worry too much about losing your job, you'll never get anything done. "The way I've always looked at it," says Wilson, "if I didn't have this job, I'd have another one soon enough."

After a decade and a half in the driver's seat at Maryland, Wilson is surprisingly modest about what he can teach other leaders. "Every dean is unique. Like the saying goes: 'If you've seen one dean, you've seen one dean.' Each of us is so different. I'm not sure it's my place to tell anyone what to do."

But when pressed, Wilson can be persuaded to reveal some of his hard-earned advice for anyone contemplating the demanding job of medical school dean—a job few people appreciate when they first move into their new office, and some may still not fully understand even on the day they move out. Given the time and the inclination, this master dean could no doubt fill several books on the rarely studied subject. Here, boiled down to their essence, are Wilson's seven time-tested suggestions for deans and other leaders.

1) Think Big

First and foremost, insists Wilson, a dean is not a figurehead but a *leader*, and from Day One, she or he must plan to think like one. Form a clear vision of what you want to accomplish and hang onto that vision no matter what is thrown your way. Don't let current conditions or limited resources block you from seeing future possibilities. If you find your new school to be sorely lacking in several key areas, wonderful!

You've hit the jack pot. With so much room to grow, you have real potential to improve things.

If, on the other hand, you are taking the helm at an already top-notch institution, resist the temptation to rest on current resources and reputation. Instead, find areas in which to stretch the school even further, such as significantly increasing community services, boosting the recruitment of minority students and faculty, and expanding research in novel areas.

Expect your vision to change over time as new opportunities arise, but don't back off on your plans simply because success is taking longer to accomplish than you originally thought. If it was so easy, someone else would probably have done it already.

Keep in mind that the bolder your vision, the fewer the people who will share it. That's because those who resist change will always be more fired up than those who support it. Faced with this reality again and again throughout his career, Wilson has drawn solace from his favorite passage of Machiavelli's *The Prince*, written more than five centuries ago:

> *There is nothing more difficult to take in hand, more perilous to conduct, or more uncertain in its success, than to take the lead in the introduction of a new order of things. Because the innovator has for enemies all those who have done well under the old conditions, and lukewarm defenders in those who may do well under the new.*

As dean, Wilson's vision for Maryland's medical school was enormous—and so was the resistance. From the start, it was an uphill battle. Faculty support for Wilson's goals ran the gamut from true believers to vocal naysayers who secretly placed bets that the new dean wouldn't last a year. Powerful department heads, thoroughly used to calling the shots and cutting their own backroom deals, faced an entirely new landscape when Wilson arrived.

> *It used to be that you walked into the dean's office, schmoozed for fifteen or twenty minutes, and then cut a personal deal of some sort—like getting the go-ahead to hire a friend or a nod for more money for one's department when the last loan had yet to be repaid. It was all very informal and random. Usually, the last person who walked out of the dean's office was the one who got the best deal.*
>
> *The first thing they discovered about the new dean was that I don't make deals. I don't care how long you schmooze me or how charming you are. Your request has to have some real justification merit based on what's best for the goals of the school. Your proposal, which needs to be in writing, has to make good business sense or good academic sense, preferably both. No amount of schmoozing was going to trump that.*

"It was a contentious time," recalls vice dean Frank Calia. "We had a campus president who was less than supportive, in part because he had felt snubbed by the medical school back in the days when he was the dental school dean. We had some politicians in the state legislature who were not entirely thrilled with everything Wilson wanted to do. And we had a group of department chairs, including a powerful clinical chair, who wanted the dean to fire me during the curriculum reform process because we were seriously rocking their boats. Of course, Wilson wouldn't budge."

Wilson's steadfast vision for the school included improving nearly ever aspect of the institution, from boosting research funding to expanding physical facilities to increasing student and faculty diversity.

But merely "thinking big" would have gotten the school nowhere without the systematic implementation of these goals, which is where Wilson's next piece of advice comes in...

2) Sell the Vision

Once you have set your sights on a clear vision for your organization, every leader must continuously and effectively *sell* that vision to others. Getting others to "buy into" your agenda is especially essential for academic leaders. With the exception of your closest allies, you must assume that everyone, everywhere you go, everyday that you are dean, needs to be persuasively and repeatedly sold. This includes other school administrators, support staff, community and business leaders, students, alumni, and most importantly, the faculty.

"Get the faculty on board and you've won half the battle," counsels Wilson. "You need to see the world from their point of view and then paint a picture of how the changes they may be fearing will benefit *them* in the long run." Faculty, students, and everyone at the school have everything to gain from a better school down the road. "People are much more likely to accept short-term pain when they understand the potential long-term gain."

Communicate, Communicate, And Communicate!

In selling the vision, each day, leaders face countless communication opportunities and challenges. In fact, Wilson says, an argument could be made that, after daily decision-making, communication is a dean's primary job description.

"You can never communicate enough" laments Wilson. Misunderstandings due to lack of information or rumored misinformation regularly occur, even in the best of circumstances. Add to this the daily conflicts that occur in every school, combined with various groups of people with agendas not identical to yours, and you have a potential recipe for real trouble. "Bad information, leading to bad reactions, leading to even less accurate information, is the norm," cautions Wilson. "And you can multiple that by a factor of ten at a medical school."

Without telling all, you must find ways to clearly and directly communicate to each person what he or she needs to know. This means countless memos, meetings, committees, letters, and formal and informal talks to let the faculty know what is going on and to get their input. All communication should remain logical, not emotional, advises Wilson. Use clear, direct language. Do not pontificate or use unnecessary jargon. Boil it down to the basics and get to the point. Keep letters and memos to one or two pages, if possible. Organize longer documents with subheads and bullets. When speaking to a group, large or small, resist the temptation to hold your listeners hostage with long-winded explanations or rambling stories, Wilson warns. "Keep it simple and cut to the chase."

Don't hide behind vague, indirect, or incomplete statements. It takes courage to communicate clearly, and that courage can be a powerful ally.

> *During my first year as dean, I addressed the medical school alumni. Alumni are an important group for any school because they have considerable resources and influence in the community, combined with the potential for real passion about your goals for the school. After my speech, then-campus president Errol Reese, who was not my strongest supporter, told me that the president of the alumni association said he understood why I was chosen for the position. I hadn't yet accomplished anything that I had come to the school to do, but simply by the way I communicated, I seemed to have given him the impression that I might actually do it.*

Throughout his years at Maryland, Wilson put a high priority on crystal clear communication. For example, after embarking on the first strategic planning process in the school's history, the dean and his team spent an entire year communicating the intent and contents of that plan to the faculty and staff. During the complex and controversial effort to revamp the school's outdated curriculum, the dean's office spent a year on the process and three years phasing in the changes to help faculty and students adjust. Later, when it became necessary to alter the rules for faculty appointment, promotion, and tenure—a highly contentious reform that, if mishandled, could have led to a vote of no-confidence for the dean—Wilson spent months clearly communicating the reasons and details of every change. When the dust finally settled, the vice-chancellor of the University System said that in his twenty-five years of experience he had never seen a policy change better communicated to the faculty.

"Communication has been vitally important to the school's success every step of the way," says Wilson. "If you want people on board, you have to make sure, on a regular basis, they understand the Who, What, When, Where, How, and Why of what you are doing and how it will affect them."

3) <u>Act Like the CEO, Not the Chairman of the Board</u>

If all a leader had to do was Think Big and Sell the Vision once, we could all go home after lunch. In reality, one's vision has to be sold and resold thousands of times, month in and month out, year after year. Not everyone will buy into your goals and many will flat out resist you every step of the way. Being an effective leader of a medical school on the move, says Wilson, means giving up any desire to act like the ever-agreeable Chairman of the Board. Instead, you must behave like a highly effective CEO of a real-world business. As the "CEO-dean" of your school, your top priority is the advancement of the institution, not winning popularity contests. A medical school dean needs a fairly thick skin under that white coat.

> *It's not the dean's job to be everybody's best friend. Faculty and staff should feel free to talk to you about any subject, but don't let them control you. Expect to piss people off, and be prepared to become angry yourself, on occasion. Whenever possible, deal with what is before you in a clear and rational manner. Explode if you must, then pull yourself together and get back to work. You can't stew in anger or let troubles continuously eat away at you if you want to get things done.*

Unlike a figurehead dean, who stands around at parties looking "dean-like," a CEO-dean is ready and willing to tackle unpopular tasks and is someone to whom others can turn when the going gets rough. Over the years, many people at Maryland say they have come to see dean Wilson, not only as the man in charge, but also as a tower of strength who the faculty, staff, and students can count on to solve seemingly impossible problems.

> *The goal is to earn and command their loyalty, trust, and respect. No matter what problems they face, you want people to be able to say, "If anyone can get us out of this mess, it's the dean."*

CEO-Deans Manage Resources

As CEO-dean of your school, it is your job to run the place like a business. You cannot allow your institution to lumber along like it's 1953 if you want to survive and thrive in today's marketplace. While your top priorities will always be the education of new physicians, the advancement of meaningful research, and cutting-edge clinical care, sustaining and expanding all that requires sound financial management.

For Wilson, that meant analyzing every source of income to the institution and managing those revenue streams for maximum benefit to the school, rather than for the benefit of individual departments, particular programs, or pet projects. Every decision pertaining to money, coming in or going out, was guided by how it positively or negatively impacted the overall mission of the entire school. Wilson was among the first in the country to implement this "Mission-based Management" approach to more efficiently run and grow the school, at a time when funding from the state was rapidly shrinking and reimbursement by insurance companies was drying up. By assessing and managing all resources with the singular goal of promoting the primary missions of the school, Wilson was able to greatly stimulate faculty productivity and research while boosting income from grants, contracts, and gifts. Mission-based Management proved so successful that it is now routinely applied in medical schools across the U.S.

As CEO-dean, Wilson fearlessly applied Mission-based Management to key revenue streams that prior deans may have considered too hot to touch, such as the Practice Plan (a corporation within the medical school which generates income from the clinical practices of the school's faculty). For years, the department chairs ran the school's Practice Plan anyway they saw fit. While deans had veto power, they had no direct management role. Money came in and was spread around at will, with no central leader making decisions that would most benefit the whole.

That was OK as long as the money flowed freely and there was plenty to go around. But by the mid 1990s, the Practice Plan faced huge challenges, with declining income relative to charges, inefficient management, and ever-increasing demands for the money. When things got bad enough, Wilson stepped in.

> *The board of directors decided to elect me president of the Practice Plan and cut out the middle guy. That's when I began to discover all the problems. It wasn't being run efficiently. We were losing money unnecessarily, outright wasting it for nothing. The process of seeing patients was inefficient and people [faculty] were not being held responsible. The first thing we did*

> is institute annual audits of each departments PA [professional association], not just to see if the dollars added up, but also to determine if what they were doing made any sense, and whether they were following all the rules and regulations required of tax-exempt organizations.

Wilson and his team discovered the school was not capturing all the charges and collections to which they were entitled, and that many common business practices were not being followed, such as effective receptionist procedures and efficient billing. In addition to the pressing need to upgrade business management and operations, there was also a real potential crisis looming regarding exactly who was in charge of the Practice Plan, the dean or the departments. Officially, there was never a question that the Practice Plan fell under the control of the school, but unofficially, the president of the Practice Plan prior to Wilson viewed it as a separate, nearly autonomous organization that benefited individual departments rather than the overall school. With Wilson as its new president, that would have to change.

One of those changes was to recruit Robert Barish, MD, head of the division of emergency medicine, to become Associate Dean for Clinical Affairs. He was a highly respected colleague among the clinical department chairs in the medical school.

Wilson insisted on individual accountability for faculty as well as staff. He instituted a "pay-for-performance" program for staff that allowed them to be rewarded financially at the end of the year for outstanding performances and to move on to another institution at the end of the year for unacceptable performances. The practice plan by-laws called for election of a president every two years. During Wilson's ten years as president, the board bi-annually rejected having an election. The practice plan saw its net collection ratio increase from 66% to 95%, and its days in arrears decline from 166 days to 53 days during Wilson's ten years as president.

CEO-Deans Take Risks

Part of behaving like an effective CEO is getting used to walking a tight rope without a net. Risk taking goes with the territory of leading a rapidly changing institution, says Wilson. "You can't play it safe, and keep moving forward. It just doesn't work that way. I certainly took a lot of risks in this job, starting with coming here. I knew it wouldn't be easy, but there were times when it started to look even worse than I had imagined."

Among the dean's riskiest moves were taking over the Practice Plan, overhauling the curriculum, demanding that the faculty boost productivity and research revenues, and replacing department chairs who failed to support the goals of the school (more on that later). Anyone of these and other changes could have completely derailed his deanship had he significantly lost faculty support.

> *The key is to keep the faculty in the loop as much as possible, and to stay in their loop as well. Make an effort to attend everything the faculty attends. You want to show that you are committed to the school and you know what is going on. If they think they know more about the daily workings of the school than you do, you won't be able to convince them that you know what you are doing, especially when you introduce change. You want to clearly communicate, not only that you are the boss, but that you <u>should</u> be the boss, because you have a game plan, and you can be counted on to tell them what to expect and to listen to their ideas.*

CEO-Deans Encourage Faculty Input

"There will always be tension between the dean's office and the faculty," says Calia. "That's only natural. The faculty want to have a say in everything, but there's a certain efficiency and pragmatism in strong leadership. If you put more and more people on committees you end up with a thousand points of view and you get nothing done. On the other hand, if you cut them out completely, the situation will become impossible. You have to find a balance, a way to get lots of faculty involvement and input without derailing the larger goals. It's been an evolving process for us. Fortunately, as strong a leader as Wilson is, he has always been open to hearing differing views. You can change his mind and he can change yours."

In addition to maintaining an open-door policy for informal discussion, Wilson boosted faculty involvement in the school by revitalizing the Faculty Council. As the official forum for faculty input on academic and educational policies, the Faculty Council had become all but dead prior to Wilson becoming dean.

> *The very first Faculty Council meeting I attended was pathetic. There couldn't have been more than twenty people in the room. I said, "This is terrible," and I was floored when an administrative assistant looked at me and said, "Oh no, this is a large group today." I thought to myself, "We have to change this. Everybody's running around with all these opinions, and yet no one shows up to discuss anything." Faculty must feel like they have a forum to air their views.*

With the dean as its chairman, the Faculty Council meets monthly, ten times a year, and includes all department chairs, the directors of all programs, elected representatives of each department, student representatives, two representatives from the Alumni Association, and two appointed assistant or associate deans. But Wilson did not stop there. "The way I do Council meetings is to invite the entire faculty. Anybody can come. We had to make sure they understood this was for them. Today, we get about 150 to 200 people to a meeting. That's what I call input!"

CEO-Deans Reel In and Restructure

Figureheads lean on the status quo; leaders look for ways to improve it. As a dean, Wilson spent many years on simultaneous reform projects, upgrading everything from the school public image to its physical facilities. While not among his most dramatic reforms, his efforts to restructure both the Cancer Center and Shock Trauma can be instructive to new deans because both cases illustrate how a CEO-dean advances his or her institution by making all activities and entities work together for the good of the school.

Prior to Wilson, the school's Cancer Center essentially operated on its own, and they liked it that way.

> *They didn't like answering to the Chairman of Medicine. If you give people the opportunity to answer to nobody, that's what they prefer. Or they want to answer to a lot of people, which is the same as answering to nobody.*

But the problem was that the Cancer Center, like many organizations without strong leadership, was not growing. As part of both the medical school and the hospital, the Cancer Center is physically located within the hospital, but its director is appointed by the medical school and all its doctors are paid by the medical school. When Wilson arrived, the Cancer Center was theoretically under the direction of the chairman of the department of Medicine, who was less than enthusiastic about supporting the Cancer Center. "He thought anything that made the Cancer Center more powerful would mean less power and control for his department over hematology, oncology, and cancer," says Handlir.

Wilson worked several ways to establish the fact that the Cancer Center is part of the medical school and was going to thrive. This was not a new idea, but one that had never actually been enforced until Wilson. Unwilling to accept business as usually, the new dean recognized that a great medical school needed a great cancer center. Because cancer crosses so many disciplines, it should not be the domain of any particular department. He also recognized the need to make leadership changes at the departmental level to fully implement the Cancer Center and the Oncology program.

Such changes do not happen overnight. Wilson boot-strapped his way up with public statements about creating a first-rate Cancer Center, medical school, campus, and hospital. He also continued behind-the-scenes talks to rally support, and he marshaled all the necessary forces—political, human, and financial—to establish a growing Cancer Center, not just in theory, but in practice. In the end, the Cancer Center had a new director and was embraced and fully supported by the medical school faculty and chairs.

The school's Shock Trauma Center is another case in point. From the beginning, Shock Trauma was an autonomous entity: Faculty salaries were not integrated with the medical school, its Practice Plan was not integrated with the medical school, and its decision-making was entirely separate.

"Many attempts were made to integrate Shock Trauma with the medical school in the hopes of improving faculty recruitment," recalls Handlir. "A medical school is like the magnet. If you want to hire the best faculty away from other institutions, they are not going to come here just to be a physician in Shock Trauma. Top-notch faculty members want to write papers, win grants, and achieve the notoriety and academic standing that comes from being associated with a medical school." Wilson understood that Shock Trauma could get better faculty if they integrated with the medical school. "But anytime the school tried to do anything in that direction," says Handlir, "the Shock Trauma people would run right to the governor or to their representatives and complain."

As CEO-dean, Wilson said this was unacceptable. In 1993, he created the first program in trauma that was also part of the medical school, involving both teaching and research. "It may seem so acceptable now, but at the time it was a huge political risk. There were so many people that if you even mentioned Shock Trauma, people would scream bloody murder that it was a takeover. It took real guts to confront that and change it."

In 1992 a new director of shock trauma was selected, who supposedly reported to Wilson and the head of the hospital system. As it turned out, his behavior indicated that he felt he reported to neither (apparently with the approval of the then campus president Reese). This too, turned out to be a blessing in disguise. His independent behavior soon ran him afoul of the governor and legislators, and soon, he was gone. Wilson subsequently recruited a young man he knew from Brooklyn, Thomas Scalea, MD. Shock trauma is now fully integrated into the medical school and is flourishing.

4) **Stand Up for Your School (and Yourself)**

Just as CEO-deans cannot please every member of the faculty and staff, neither can they always please their superiors. "Don't be afraid to stand up to your boss when you feel it is necessary," suggests Wilson. It is unlikely that anyone on campus, regardless of their position, fully appreciates the needs and potentials of the medical school better than you do. "They hired you to protect and promote your institution, not acquiesce to people who don't grasp what's going on."

Work towards developing a constructive process to discuss and work out your differences with your boss, other deans, the president of the campus, or whomever may not understand what you are doing with the school. Rational, direct communication and mutual respect for your differing responsibilities and demands will go a long way to help you get your points across.

If necessary, be willing to go up the line to your boss's boss or to community leaders and state legislators to win support. Remember, you are advancing the best interests of the school, which is exactly what they hired you to do.

Fight Back

While standing up to your boss, you may also find it necessary to defend yourself against various rumors, detractors, and even law suits.

> *As dean of the medical school, I got sued all over the place. I got sued for this; I got sued for that. The very first week I was dean, I was sued by some student who was thrown out for cheating. What the person thought they might gain from that, I have no idea. Nobody ever wins these things; everybody loses. You've got to give it time and attention you could be putting elsewhere. You have to deal with the lawyers; you have to give depositions—all of it. In the end, they never win, but it eats up a lot of your time.*

One particularly annoying case involved a thirty-seven-year-old man who was denied acceptance to the medical school because his application did not meet school standards. But that didn't stop him from filing a lawsuit in 1998 against both the university and the dean for—of all things—reverse discrimination. Claiming that the school had turned him away because he was not a member of a minority, he told the Baltimore Sun, "If you're a white guy and all you've tried to do is work hard and be honest, you can't get in."

The case caught the attention of a conservative, anti-affirmative action group in Washington, who immediately took up the cause of hammering the nation's first African-American dean of a majority school. The group tried to help the rejected applicant show a pattern at the school, under Wilson's deanship, of favoring black applicants over whites. The case, of course, was dismissed.

> *The judge went out of his way to say the man was simply not qualified to get into <u>any</u> medical school, period. Why would a medical school want to admit somebody who didn't do very well*

in college, who couldn't get even one decent letter of recommendation, and who made derogatory remarks about physicians? The fact was he didn't get into any of the schools to which he applied in the United States, nor should he.

More importantly, the judge found no credible evidence of reverse discrimination at the school, but the groundless charges lingered like a cloud over the dean's office because they voiced what some whites on campus had privately assumed: that Maryland's first black dean unfairly favored blacks over whites.

"Most of us knew that was absolutely, flat-out not true," says Calia, who happens to be white. "Wilson is probably the most fair guy I have ever met, and I know an awfully lot of very fair people."

But that didn't stop many people from thinking the worst. "Some people's most racist tendencies came out in relation to Don Wilson," recalls Sylvan Frieman, MD, who was chairman of the Medical Alumni Association at that time. "It wasn't organized, but it was pervasive. You could just feel it. The word was going around that Wilson wanted to make this a black medical school. That was so completely untrue. The fact was, if there was any racial discrimination going on, it was not *by* the dean, but against him. Wilson fought a hell of a racial barrier here from Day One. And in return, he has been nothing but fair and open and honest with everybody."

For his part, Wilson has ignored it all as much as possible. Borrowing a quote from the dean of Yale University School of Medicine, Wilson said in his 1995 State of the School address, "In order to cope, deans must possess the craftiness of Machiavelli, the infinite wisdom of Confucius, and fiscal acumen of J.P. Morgan."

Take the High Road

Wilson implores all academic leaders to make every effort to do the right thing and think about others.

> *Each year I become more dismayed by people who seem to have as their only consideration themselves and what they can do for themselves, as opposed to how their actions and interactions may impact others and naturally help others. I tell folks starting out in academic medicine, take the high road. Don't ever try to undermine another individual. Don't ever purposely hurt another individual. I sometimes use the term, what goes around comes around, and it does to a great extent, although we do often see people who have been jerks all their lives and still get ahead. But on balance, being considerate of others and being willing to help others when you can will probably be more beneficial to you than being selfish and unwilling to help anybody unless they can help you in return. At the end of the day, or at the end of your life, you're not going to regret having done the right thing. Don't ever circum to the lowest common denominator. Take the high road, and if you're lucky, others will follow you.*

"Wilson stood his ground," recalls Handlir. "He didn't just improve our finances and our research output; he took on some of the longest-standing, nastiest cultural and attitudinal issues at this school. It took a while, but he fundamentally changed this place for the better. At this point, his worse detractors have either come around and joined the rest of us, or left town."

5) **Pick Your Battles**

Standing firm and above the fray sometimes also requires leaders to practice the fine art of strategic compromise. "Pick your battles," Wilson advises. Many times, the exact details of how and when something occurs or does not occur really doesn't matter all that much to the overall outcome. Instead of viewing compromise as an obstacle to your goals, think of it as a tool for moving the school forward. "Whenever it doesn't cost you too much to let people have what they want, do so. You can use that good will later to get what you want. If the compromise does cost you something, make sure you negotiate something even better for it in return."

As a strong leader, it is to your advantage to treat all people, even your adversaries, with respect. If you have to relieve someone of their duties, says Wilson, find a way to do so that leaves their dignity intact. "Allow people to save face. They will usually go away quietly, and if they happen to go nuts, they won't get a following of supporters."

No matter what the circumstances, it never pays to go after someone in revenge, no matter how richly you may feel they deserve it.

> *In all of my years, I can say that I have never destroyed anyone, even though there are many who earned it. For cause, I have had numerous opportunities to take negative actions against individuals, and in almost all instances, I have refused to respond to the insult and have simply allowed these people to "get away."*
>
> *People around me will say, "You didn't do anything to so-and-so?" and I can look at them and say, "No, I didn't do anything to that person." If he or she failed, they failed entirely on their own. By and large, sooner or later, all these people have either self-destructed or led inconsequential lives. It's really not necessary to go after people. Nasty people usually end up having nasty events follow them. And what's most important, it's not on my conscience and I don't have to worry about it.*

Whenever possible, says Wilson, avoid any opportunity to create an enemy. "In the long run, it will do neither of you a bit of good."

Sometimes, however, enemies are impossible to avoid...

Wilson's Way

"You're Fired!"

At times it becomes necessary to remove leaders from their position. The chairman of medicine was not able to get on board with the new vision of the school of medicine. Wilson described him as "a 1960s chair that was unwilling or unable to change."

"Wilson and Morton Rapoport, MD, the head of the hospital met with the chairman of medicine to inform him that he was not on the same wave length regarding institutional goals, and therefore, a change needed to be made. They told him to send a letter of resignation, and they would throw him a party and make it all look like it was his idea. He said thank you and left Wilson's office. A day or two later, while the dean was off at a meeting on the West Coast, Wilson got a call from one of his associates, saying the soon-to-be-former chairman was running around, secretly meeting with the other department chairs, trying to foment problems, and telling people he had been inappropriately dismissed by the dean and the faculty had to do something about it.

"With some of the department heads, it got ugly," recalls Tyson Tilden. "There were people who openly circulated vile, racially biased cartoons. One was a Doonesbury cartoon in which a guy was asking someone, 'Can you do this job?' and they had inked the guy black and added the wording 'Don can't do that.' Garry Trudeau could get them for plagiarism."

> *The fact that the chairman of medicine appeared to be bent on fomenting dissent was not all that important to me. But the fact that he would not get on board and support the direction in which the School of Medicine was going—that was a very significant problem.*
>
> *When I got back, I called him on the phone and I said, "Effective this minute, you are no longer chair of the department of medicine. All authority that you have for running the department is hereby rescinded, etc., etc. In other words, you're fired."*

He tried to sue me in Baltimore County, rather than Baltimore City. The medical school doesn't have anything in Baltimore County. The hospital has one section, Kernan Hospital, in Baltimore County, so his lawyers tried to use that as an excuse to bring the lawsuit in Baltimore County where you get a different kind of jury, mostly white. Anyway, he lost. The judge just looked at the case and said, "You lose." Then he appealed it to the Appellate Court where he lost again. At one point, he said he was going to try to appeal it to the U.S. Supreme Court, which he didn't.

Faculty are funny. Even if they do not like the current situation, they frequently support the status quo initially rather than embrace change. Many people in the department of medicine did not agree with the current leadership, but they still rallied around him when they heard he was being removed. I told them we would have a new department chair and I appointed the vice dean Frank Calia, MD. Within two years we had a highly qualified permanent chair William Henrich, MD, who is now himself a medical school dean. Nobody quit. Actually, almost everybody was quite happy.

That former chair, by the way, is still here in a faculty position. Tenure is interesting.

Another major department chair found it difficult to accept the curricular changes that were occurring in the medical school. This particular department chair was extraordinarily resistant to changing the curriculum. He thought he knew best how to educate students, exactly how many weeks he needed to teach this and that, and how it should all be done. He voiced his opinions quite loudly, which was fine. But then after he left the meetings where clear decisions had been made, he would continue his negative campaign. I had him come into my office and I told him that had to change. I said, "You may not like it, but once decisions have been reached by the processes that we use,

> *as a member of my executive team, you have to support those decisions." He said "OK."*
>
> *But then we had a meeting of the Executive Committee where we presented our plans, and the chairman decided to speak vehemently against our agreed-upon curriculum reforms. That was not acceptable, so I asked him to step down. He said, "You can't do that!" and I said, "Oh, yes, I can." In the Executive Committee meeting you don't upstage your dean. Period. He quite graciously retired.*

Under entirely different circumstances, Wilson also removed the chairman of the Department of Surgery. In this case, it was not a question of loyalty or disrespect, but a matter of a good person no longer functioning effectively in his job. "It wasn't an age issue," says Handlir, "He just lost his edge to manage his department and he then lost confidence of the faculty." Wilson moved him to an administrative position that allowed the man to retain self-respect. Unfortunately, he was unable to handle that job as well, and eventually, Wilson gently let him go.

That's the kind of a leader and physician Wilson is, says Tyson Tilden. "Whether he kicks butt or uses sugar and quiet persuasion, he gets the job done. As a physician or as a leader, you go in to see him and he says, 'This is not going to hurt—Did it?' And just like that, it's all done before you have a chance to even think about the pain."

Replacing several powerful department chairs with more effective and cooperative leaders extinguished any remaining fantasies of mutiny by the faculty.

> *In the end it was great because people saw that the dean could get rid of the chairman of medicine <u>and</u> the chairman of surgery—and survive it. After that, nobody wanted to mess with the dean any more.*

6) Recruit Good People

Leaders make their lasting marks by the hands of highly capable people they hire and inspire to share their vision and turn dreams into realities. Therefore, it is vitally important throughout your deanship to find the right individuals for the right jobs at the right time—and then *get out of their way* and let them do their work.

"You cannot micromanage your way to success," says Wilson. "With the right people, you shouldn't have to."

A dean's role is often part cheerleader, part firefighter, part orchestra conductor, and part human resource manager. "You have to find a balance," says Wilson. "You have to be involved and you have to be detached."

Associate dean for resource management, Greg Handlir, who has seen lots of people come and go in his three decades at the school, believes that a corner stone of Wilson's record-breaking success has been his ability to recruit top faculty and staff. "It has been especially important that he got the best possible department chairs. Not just strong academicians, but people who were also strong leaders and strong managers. It's a fundamental mark of a true leader when they hire strong lieutenants and others who can step up to the plate, should it become necessary. Wilson has systematically surrounded himself with excellent people at every level. It's been a real team philosophy."

In building your team, Wilson suggests looking beyond the usual factors that make potential employees seem attractive. For example, he says to try to avoid "resume builders," people who come in for relatively short periods of time for the prime purpose of adding your institution to their CVs, as they climb the ladder toward another position. "You want people who will put the broader, longer-range goals of the institution ahead of their own short-term agendas to position themselves for the next job. That, of course, is easier said than done."

It's also wise to look for potential, not just experience. Both are ideal, but often potential is worth more in the long run. Likewise, intangibles such as enthusiasm and reliability can be more valuable to you than resume headlines.

In the hunt for diamonds, here is Wilson's Top Ten Wish List for recruiting the best and the brightest:

- **Smart**. Intelligent people simply make better work colleagues than less intelligent people, but don't assume knowledge equals intelligence. Bright, motivated people can be taught. Sometimes the best people don't have long resumes.
- **Highly Competent in Their Area of Expertise**. Preferably, better at whatever it is that they do than you would be in that job.
- **Share Your Vision**. Ideally, they should understand what is in the best interest of the school and use these broader goals to guide their daily actions.
- **Self-starter**. Nothing beats an independent, self-motivated team player who shares your vision and can initiate new ways to get there, within their area of control.
- **Outgoing**. Good "people skills" are vital, including competent oral and written communication, active listening, and the ability to collaborate and work well with others.
- **Disciplined**. It takes a lot of time and effort to build a dream. Over the long haul, hard work and dedication trump creative genius. (All three would be lovely.)
- **Flexible**. Change is the one thing we can count on in life. The ability to adapt to an ever-changing environment limits stress and promotes productivity. People who cannot go with the flow may become liabilities down the road.
- **Honest**. No lie is acceptable when you're trying to accomplish something complex and important. Your leadership decisions depend on accurate information and the people who are courageous enough to give it to you.

- **Trustworthy**. Honesty alone is not enough. You don't want someone to steal you blind and then truthfully confess. You need to know you can count on every member of your team, every time, to do what they say.
- **Loyal**. Essential and non-negotiable.

7) Know When to Move On

After you Think Big, Sell the Vision, Act like a CEO, Stand Up for Your School, Pick Your Battles, and Recruit Good People, your final leadership move is knowing when enough is enough.

The average medical school dean quits in less than five years, hardly enough time to get anything significant done. Don't take the job if your heart is not in it. Find a position in which you can have a real impact and stick around a while to see it through.

Exactly how long to stay, however, may not be immediately obvious, especially after years of fighting the good fight. On the subject of moving on, Wilson enjoys recounting the words of an outstanding academic chairman who once said many leaders suffer from "mural dyslexia," or "How can you read the handwriting on the wall when the SOBs always have your back up against it?"

Still, there comes a time when every leader has to say enough is enough, either because you can make no headway, or because you have successfully gone as far as you can reasonably go. Even the most dedicated deans must eventually plan and execute their exit strategies.

Looking Forward to Looking Back

With all that Dean Wilson has managed to accomplish, often under the most difficult of circumstances, if he had the chance, would he do it all again?

> *Frankly, I don't know if I would. It's been a fishbowl job from Day One, with everybody watching and some people waiting for*

me to screw up. Being dean is easy if all you want to do is be a good caretaker and set yourself on auto-pilot. But if you want to make some real changes, it takes a lot out of you. I could have left the counterproductive department chairs in place; I could have allowed the Practice Plan to continue losing money; I could have left the outdated curriculum alone. But then we wouldn't have the school we have today.

It's human nature to think of change as negative. People will resist you every step of the way and the negativity can bring you down, if you let it. Every once in while I think to myself, "I must be crazy to be here, trying to cram twenty hours of work into a fifteen-hour workday, trying to do the impossible while being pushed and pulled in so many different directions—all the calls and the meetings, all the requests from the state legislature, the university, the media, the unrealistic demands, the prima donna department chairs, dealing with some lazy employees and some idiotic faculty (the kind of people who couldn't make a decision if their life depended on it, but they want to be involved.)" All of it. It's relentless. I'd say maybe one day out of twenty, I actually had a great day at work. But if you look around at what we've built, it feels pretty damn good.

It feels pretty good to many other university leaders, as well. "Wilson's commitment to education, research, and service is unparalleled," gushes the normally reserved University of Maryland, Baltimore campus president David J. Ramsay, DM, DPhil., his genuine affection for Wilson shining through his stayed British accent. "He will continue to have a significant impact here, long after he retires."

University System of Maryland Chancellor William Kirwan, PhD., agrees. "Dr. Wilson was the right man at the right time for our medical school. His vision has led the University of Maryland School of Medicine into the top echelon of American medical schools. That is a legacy only a privileged few can boast."

If you want to really understand what the school has gained under Wilson's firm leadership, says Handlir, "just take a moment to contemplate what we would *not* have now, if we did not have Don Wilson since 1991. For starters, we would not have had one, never mind two formal strategic plans—with every item, by the way, fully accomplished. We would not have an associate dean of research and an associate dean of clinical affairs, two very key appointments. We would not have the tremendous information technology, or the excellent relationships with the state legislature and the Alumni Association and the Hospital. We would not have the Office of Development, which has brought us millions of dollars. We would not have the Health Sciences I facility, much less Health Sciences II. I could go on and on. The bottom line is that Wilson has made this one of the finest, most productive and successful medical institutions in the country. I am so proud to have been part of the team."

* * *

On an overcast day at the end of 2005, a visitor asked dean Wilson what's next. Pausing for a moment to view the sprawling campus from his 14th floor windows, his once jet-black hair now entirely grey from fifteen years of doing the impossible, the sixty-nine-year-old master dean quickly shot off an ambitious list of future projects: more research and clinical buildings, more fund raising activities, and plans for a year-long celebration when the nation's oldest public medical school marks its 200th birthday in 2007.

"At some point, you have to figure out when you're done," he said abruptly, turning toward his visitor with that piercing glare of unadulterated honesty that only Donald Wilson can deliver.

"I think I'm done."

And on September 1, 2006, Donald E. Wilson—the nation's first African American dean of a majority medical school; the dynamic leader who built the University of Maryland School of Medicine into a powerhouse of research, education, and leading-edge clinical care; the man who outfoxed his white racist landlord in 1963 Nebraska when others might have simply turned away; the pioneering researcher; the teacher; the mentor; the black medical school student in a sea of white coats and white faces; the young brown boy with a big, bold American dream to be a doctor someday—packed up his papers and books in the dean's office on the 14th floor, bid his colleagues farewell, and went home.

This year, Wilson stepped down as the director of the University of Maryland's Program in Minority Health and Health Disparities Research and Education, an organization he created while dean and is dedicated to keeping alive after he's gone.

"There's still so much work to be done."

Wilson with family, left to right Monique, Sean and wife Patricia at unveiling of official portrait honoring his retirement in 2006

CHAPTER 10

Wilson's Way: Win, Don't Whine
Ten Success Secrets for Everyone, Everywhere

By Donald E. Wilson, MD

That's life, that's what people say
You're riding high in April, shot down in May
But I know I'm gonna change that tune
When I'm back on top in June

That's life, funny as it seems
Some people get their kicks, steppin' on dreams
But I don't let it get me down
'Cause this ol' world keeps getting around

I've been a puppet, a pauper, a pirate, a poet, a pawn and a king
I've been up and down and over and out, and I know one thing
Each time I find myself flat on my face
I pick myself up and get back in the race

That's life, I can't deny it
I thought of quitting, but my heart just won't buy it

> ***And if I didn't think it was worth a try***
> ***I'd roll myself up in a big ball and die***
> *"That's Life"*
> By Dean Kay and Kelly Gordan

Thank you for reading about my life and times. We all know there's a lot more to any story than can fit between the covers of a book, but if I had to boil it all down to just a few pages, I say there are ten proven principles for winning, especially if you are a minority trying to win in a white man's world. I do not mean to be disrespectful, but the truth of the matter is that we all still live in a white man's world, whether you like it or not, and you might as well get on with your life. No matter what your race, your gender, your background, or your education, no matter what your current abilities, your challenges, or your long-range goals, anyone—and I really do mean *anyone*—can boost their odds for personal and professional success by consistently applying these ten strategies.

Depending on your temperament, values, intelligence, and work ethic, you will probably find some of these easier than others to put into action. Observe yourself. Often the ones you find the most difficult to apply daily are precisely the areas of your life which need the most attention. In other words, the harder it is, the more you need to do it.

Some people might say I've been lucky. Certainly, I was very fortunate to be raised by Rivers and Licine Wilson. I was also very fortunate to have gone to a college-preparatory high school, which set the stage for me to attend Harvard and Tufts. And certainly, I was fortunate to have been born with above average intelligence and relatively good health. In many important ways, the dice have rolled in my favor.

On the other hand, I was born African American in a predominantly white, predominantly racist nation, in 1936, not exactly at a time of great social justice and equal opportunity for all. A few years before I was born, my father fled South Carolina to avoid being lynched. Setting up their first home in Massachusetts, my parents were as poor as a couple of tin cans, at least when they started out. And before my sister and I graduated from high school, no one in my family had ever even made it through grammar school, let alone went on to college and medical school.

Throughout my life, at nearly every bump and turn and fork in the road, there were no role models to guide me, no mentors to show me the ropes or open the doors. It is not an exaggeration to say that at every step of the way, from kindergarten to medical school and beyond, I've had to blaze my own trail.

So, was I lucky? You bet I was lucky! But I also *made* much of my own luck—and so can you.

Wilson's Way #1: Have a Vision for Where You Want to Go

This much I know: If you don't know where you're going, odds are very good that you will not get there. Great accomplishments don't happen by accident. Knowing where you want to go is always the starting point for any future success. You simply cannot skip this step and expect to get anywhere. Indeed, without a vision of what you want, how will you recognize it if you achieve it? Even if someone handed you everything on a silver platter, without a vision how would you use it?

A vision is a clear, mental image of a desired goal. Your vision may be relatively modest, or it may be quite ambitious, requiring many intermediate steps and involving many people over many years. Whatever you pick, expect your vision to change and grow over time.

For example, as a boy, I once worked in a bowling alley after school, on weekends, and during the summer months. My job was to sit behind the pins as the ball rolled down the alley, run for cover as the pins flew through the air, set the pins back up the moment they hit the ground, and roll the ball back down the alley to the customer. My goal was to get out there as quickly as possible and stand those pins up as fast as I could without getting whacked by ball or pins. It may sound as simple and as boring as watching grass grows, but in fact, there was a real art to it.

There was another boy who had been working the pins a lot longer than I, and he was good, very good. He moved around the pins like liquid light, almost like a dance. At that time and in that situation, that dance was vision enough for me. Certainly, I did not plan to spend the rest of my life setting up bowling pins, but that was the task at hand and when I showed up for work, I gave it my all. I never did get as good as that other kid, but right up to the day I set my last pin, I tried my best to move like liquid light.

Later, as the head of my church debate team, my goals were obviously quite different. My vision in that situation was to win every argument, and generally, I did. Losing simply did not fit into my thinking; therefore, I never let it cross my mind. If you spend too much time worrying about failure, you are messing with your vision.

One's vision may be short-term, long-term, or very long-term. As a young boy with my heart set on becoming a doctor, I knew that getting into and through medical school was going to take quite a bit longer than learning to set bowling pins or win debates. People sometimes ask me how it was that a nine-year-old could have set such a long-range goal and stick with it. Frankly, I have never been sure how to answer that question. All I know is, without a long-term goal, I would not have MD after my name today.

Sometimes, one's vision is too small. It's a good idea, every once in a while, to exercise the right to stretch your own vision. Even if your goal is fairly hefty, make it a habit to consider enlargement. When I first came to the University of Maryland, my initial goal was to survive the state budget cuts. Almost immediately, I stretched this vision to include raising millions of dollars to support the medical school and building a new facility to expand research funding. When we saw that was being accomplished, we then added curricular reform. Of course, some of the improvements we envisioned for the school have not yet come to pass. But I know for a fact that without vision, next to none of it would have occurred.

One way to get in the habit of stretching your vision is to occasionally help someone else stretch theirs. When I first met Dolores, she was a laboratory technician in my research lab. She was good at her job and her goal was to become even better at it. That would have been enough for someone else, but I could see that Dolores's vision for herself was too limited. It soon became obvious to me that Dolores was bright, committed, and had a strong work ethic—perfect doctor material.

When I first suggested that she consider becoming a physician, Dolores was downright amused. The idea seemed preposterous to her. But I persisted, and after a while my bright lab technician stopped laughing and began hearing what I was saying. Today Dolores is a board-certified, practicing Internist.

Some visions are too big for a particular time frame. If time runs out before your vision materializes, don't give up simply because some arbitrary time period expires. Keep working until you make it happen or you rethink your goals and get yourself another vision.

Some goals are not only too ambitious for a particular time frame, they are too big to achieve in one lifetime. Nonetheless, with sustained vision and persistent action, some progress—perhaps even some significant progress—can be made. Think of the visions held fast by people like Martin Luther King, Jr. and Mahatma Gandhi. With less star power, but not necessarily less dedication, think of the impact that certain teachers, community leaders, parents, and others may have had in your life, perhaps without you realizing their influence at the time. Guided by ideals that transcend immediate rewards, such people touch the lives of many, sometimes across generations.

Don't assume that you cannot create a life that benefits both you and the larger community around you. Earning a good income doesn't necessarily mean turning your back on the world; and doing good works needn't require a vow of poverty. For people with a lot to give, careers in medicine, especially academic medicine, can be especially rewarding.

Whatever you pick set your *own* goals, not the goals others may set for you. Fall in love with your vision and assume you will succeed. Plan on it, work towards it, and make it happen.

If you don't know what you want achieve and you currently don't have a clear goal, start by aiming to be the very best at whatever you are doing right now. Stretch yourself to strive for excellence. You can do much more than you think, and when you do, you may just impress yourself enough to get yourself a vision.

Wilson's Way #2: Work Hard

If you're looking for a short cut around hard work, here it is: There isn't any. Unless you are born into a royal family in a fantasy land of milk, honey, and perfect weather, there is simply no substitute for hard work and dedication, no way around the fact that you have to get up every morning and put in the hours it takes to get where you want to go. The sooner you accept this fact and get to work, the faster you will be on your way.

In addition to moving you closer to your goals, a side benefit of persistent hard work is that it will leave you very little time to sit around and feel sorry for yourself. In fact, productive, hard work is the single best way to overcome negativity and feel more in control of your life.

I find it interesting how many bright and ambitious people don't realize that sustained success requires on-going, hard work. As dean of a medical school, I was sometimes visited by people who came into my office, complaining that they were overwhelmed, that they didn't have enough time to do this or to get that done, and so forth. I always asked them, "How many hours a week are you working?" If they said anything less than sixty, I told them they were not putting in the time it takes to succeed. It's not that they didn't have enough time; it's that they were not willing to work hard enough. If you have a big vision, you simply cannot work forty hours a week and expect to achieve it.

Working hard, therefore, involves another key principle for success: delayed gratification. You have to get used to putting off some immediate fun and relaxation in exchange for the deep satisfaction that comes from making real progress toward your goals. Get used to working hard, and in time, the work itself will become gratifying because you know it is taking you where you want to go.

In his 1975 book *The Greatest*, Mohamed Ali explains that, "Champions are made from something they have deep inside: a desire, a dream, a vision." They have to have last minute stamina; they have to be a little faster; they have to have the skill and the will. But the will must be stronger than the skill."

The "will" Ali talks about is what separates the winners from the losers. The will is the on-going drive that becomes countless daily decisions to keep working. Whatever your goal or vision, you must not sit idly by merely admiring it. You must infuse your vision with *massive sustained action*. You must wake up everyday, get dressed, and get to work.

Wilson's Way #3: Take Risks

The truth is, we really could stop right here, after "Have a Vision" and "Work Hard," and you'd have most of what you need to create a successful life. But if you want to really be in the driver's seat, there is a bit more fine-tuning beyond setting goals and working your tail off to reach them. You also need to know when to play it safe and when to go for broke. Successful risk-taking is part intuition, part experience, and the truth is I can't really give you either of these. But I can tell you that, more often than not, you are better off taking a risk than risking a lost opportunity. Obviously, there are important exceptions to this general rule, but other than in life and death situations, I have found that taking risks often leads to unexpected benefits, even when it does not directly help you achieve the original goals.

Throughout my years, I have taken risks in my personal and professional life, and they have paid off in many ways. For example, in 1971 when I was at the Brooklyn Hospital, I was offered the position of chief of gastroenterology. It would have been comfortable, but it did not fit in with my vision of achieving prominence in academic medicine. I was offered positions at Yale, Columbia, and University of Illinois. Much to the surprise of many of my colleagues, I chose Illinois. Although Illinois was the least prominent in stature and had the greatest downside risk to me personally, the upside potential far exceeded these risks. History proved that decision to be the best one.

Many times, what may seem to be a roadblock can turn out to be an open door. In 1964 when I was seeking a gastroenterology fellowship, I applied to my medical school training program. The program director did not find me to be attractive enough and did not offer me a position. That really pissed me off. Instead, I ended up working with the renowned Thomas Chalmers, an expert in liver disease. Within eight years, I ended up directing my own training program in gastroenterology at Illinois, and I became a full professor before the Tufts program director who rejected me achieved that honor.

Like knowing when to take risks, knowing where and when to look for opportunities also comes with experience. Occasionally, opportunity may come knocking on your door, but more often than not, you have to go out and hunt it down. Over time, you will develop an intuition or "gut feeling" that can help you identify and capitalize on opportunities as they arise. In the meantime, you can start immediately by training yourself to actively look for opportunities in every situation. Train yourself to look for ways to turn a negative into a positive, or a positive into an even bigger success. Remember, don't wait around for good things to happen; get out there and *make* them happen.

Win or lose, taking a calculated, rational risk is almost always a smart move. Either you take the risk and succeed, leading you closer to your goal, or you take the risk and fail, giving you the satisfaction of having tried that route and the knowledge of what not to do next time.

At the very least, risk-taking helps you avoid asking yourself "what if." Keep in mind that most regrets at the end of one's life are about lost opportunities, not about having given something your best shot. Quite often, the biggest risk of all is to try to play it safe.

Wilson's Way #4: Be Honest

Honesty contains power that you can use to your advantage. You certainly needn't tell everything to everybody. In fact, in many situations, the less said the better. But when you do speak, make it a habit to tell the truth. Being chronically honest has several big advantages. First, it is respectful to yourself and others. It gives people the information they need to do what they need to do, which may include helping you. Secondly, telling the truth is far easier than lying because you don't have to remember which fabrication you told whom. Lies have a way of coming back to you like pigeons, and the accompanying mess that it entails. And third, people are far more likely to tell *you* the truth when you are straight with them.

As dean, I could not always tell people what they wanted to hear. Many times, I had to say No when they wanted me to say yes. Many times, I had to reveal important information or give feedback that was not particularly pleasing to the recipient. Being honest requires a bit of a thick skin. In the long run, the truth is usually far more valuable to all concerned than simply being "nice."

Of course, there is no good reason not to be tactful whenever possible. Never use the excuse of honesty to purposely harm or humiliate someone else. No one benefits from reckless truth-telling done merely to make you look or feel superior. Even when you are angry, avoid the temptation to defeat anyone, no matter how richly you feel they may deserve it. Always give people the opportunity to save face. It's better for them and it's better for you. Sooner or later, that individual will most likely hang himself on his own, without you getting involved. There's no point in creating an enemy.

If you have to fire someone, which I occasionally have had to do, find a way to do so confidentially and without emotion. Firing someone is really not personal for either of you. More often than you might think, giving someone the opportunity to leave a position in which they are not doing well comes as a relief to them and is a plus for the organization.

Wilson's Way #5: Don't Try to Please Everyone

Closely related to finding the courage to be honest is the willingness to ruffle a few feathers once in awhile. You simply cannot please all of the people all of the time, especially if you are trying to create something new. Most people don't like change, and you can count on a certain level of resistance at every step of the way. Get used to it. Some objections may include valid points worthy of your consideration. Or not. Listen to what others have to say, but do not concern yourself with being liked. It may be tempting to placate complainers simply to keep the peace. Resist that temptation. Remember, life is not a popularity contest; focus on your goals.

Understand this: The larger your vision, the more resistance you will encounter. Albert Einstein once said, "Great spirits often encounter violent opposition from mediocre minds." The greater your commitments and responsibilities, the more frequently you will have to make tough, unpopular decisions that will irritate some people in order to bring about positive change that benefits the whole. If you want to be leader, you cannot behave like the chairman of the board. Your job is not to agree with everyone, but to rally others to buy into your vision. I am not giving you a license to be obnoxious or rude. There is rarely justification for that. I am asking you to find the courage to stand up for what you believe, even if you have to stand alone.

Like General Colin L. Powel says in his recent biography, being responsible sometimes includes pissing people off:

> *Good leadership involves responsibility to the group, which means that some people will be angry at your actions and decisions. It's inevitable, if you are honorable. Trying to get everyone to like you is a sign of mediocrity: you'll avoid the tough decisions, you'll avoid confronting the people who need confronting ... Ironically, by procrastinating on the difficult choices, by trying not to get anyone mad, and treating everyone equally*

nicely, regardless of their contributions, you'll simply ensure that the only people you'll wind up angering are the most creative and productive people in the organization.

Along with not trying to please everyone, it is also important not to allow people to take advantage of you—unless, of course, it is to your advantage to let them do so.

Wilson's Way #6: Know Your Strengths and Weaknesses

Having big dreams, bold vision, and the courage, persistence, and work ethic to see it through doesn't mean you walk on water. Be realistic about who you are and what you can actually do. In each situation and throughout your career, make an ongoing effort to identify your strengths and weaknesses. Knowing what you can do well will help you stay on track and move forward when others tell you to turn back. Knowing your weaknesses is even more important because these are the areas in which you will most likely run into trouble if you try to go alone. Knowing your weaknesses will help you identify the people who will be the most helpful to you, whether they be potential employees, colleagues, bosses, or mentors. A good understanding of your weaknesses will help you identify those complimentary strengths in others, stop any urges to micro-manage, and get you the help you need when you need it.

All this may seems terribly obvious, hardly worth mentioning. Yet, more often than not, many highly capable people fail to reach their goals simply because they have not clearly identified their basic strengths and weaknesses, the later being their main blind spot. When you fail to face what you cannot do well, you run the risk of trying to do it yourself. This is as true at the top of the ladder as it is on the first rung of your career.

Back in 1993, there was a book called *The Peter Principle*, in which author Laurance J. Peter pointed out that sometimes people in high positions have "risen to the level of their incompetence." The author contends that many organizations promote employees until they reach jobs they cannot do well, driving their colleagues crazy and dragging down productivity across the board. While the book concentrates on the corporate structures that lead to this problem, the deeper cause is rooted in inaccurate personal assessments of one's own competency. Remember, no matter who promotes you or passes you by, *you* are the one who is ultimately responsible for figuring out what you are good at and what you need help with.

We all want to see ourselves in the best light, but turning a blind eye on your own limitations will not serve you. Be realistic about what you can do, and get out there and do it. Think of your weaknesses not as faults but as opportunities for others to help you move you closer to your goals. Whatever you are trying to achieve, the sooner you accurately assess your strengths and weaknesses, the better.

Wilson's Way #7: Surround Yourself with Good People

At every stage of life, surround yourself with positive, honest, take-action people. Bypass the whiners, freeloaders, and folks who just want to coast. Certainly, it is charitable to offer your support to others who cannot do for themselves. Just make sure that *you* are the one who is doing the choosing, and don't let others decide who gets to lean on you. This is essential, whether you are working at a gas station or designing a space station. Whatever your task, find people who share your vision or at least won't knock it, people who compliment your weaker areas, and who are better than you at whatever they do.

If you are a student struggling in certain subject areas, get tutoring help and cultivate friendships with successful peers. If you are an entrepreneur drowning in office papers, hire a professional organizer. If you are a business executive or academic leader with big ideas, but you are not especially detail oriented, surround yourself with meticulously accurate people who share your commitment to your goals.

I also suggest that you pick your bosses carefully. Don't agree to work for people who will try to hold you back, unless you can see a way to succeed despite them. Throughout my career, I have passed up positions based on my assessment of my potential superiors. I have also taken jobs, fully knowing I would have to deal with a difficult boss, when I thought I might be able to work around them.

If you are in a position to hire others, go out of your way to choose people who are bright, motivated, honest, and potentially loyal. Don't be swayed to hire the almost-right person simply because their resume looks good. Better to train a somewhat less experienced person than to hire someone who doesn't have the heart, brains, or drive to roll up their sleeves and get to work. Employees and colleagues can learn as they go, but it's impossible to change someone's basic intelligence, morality, or work ethic.

Throughout my career, I've looked for people who are loyal, good at what they do, supportive of my vision, and willing to represent me in a positive light to others. My best hires have been people who had all these traits, as well as strengths that complement areas in which I am less strong.

After you surround yourself with good people who know more than you in their areas of expertise, get out of their way and let them do their work. Resist any urges to micro-manage or you may end up doing everyone else's job, probably rather poorly. Keep your door open to answer questions and act as a sounding board for their ideas, but do not block them from doing what you have hired them to do.

If you are just starting out in your career, seek out successful role models within your field. If possible, find and approach potential mentors until you find one you can learn from directly. If that is not possible, identify someone you can watch from a distance. Throughout my schooling and early career, I never saw a single African American physician in academic medicine. Although I managed to find my own way, I cannot help but wonder what my life might have been like had I enjoyed the far-reaching benefits of a real mentor. Studies show that the value of mentors and role models, especially for people pursuing careers never before attempted by anyone in their families, is quite significant. Mentors not only provide information and support for making career choices, they also help open doors, provide access to powerful people, and offer experienced advice as you negotiate the maze of big and small decisions along the way.

Mentors don't fall from the sky; you have to go out and get one. Actively look for potential mentors at school, on the job, in your religious community, within clubs and associations, online, and in the media. If your current mentor is not providing the help and support you need, get yourself a new one. Sometimes an accomplished friend or an inspiring teacher can be just as powerful as a formal career mentor.

Wilson's Way #8: Put Yourself in the Other Guy's Shoes

Temporarily putting aside your own views and step into someone else's shoes will do you a world of good. This is important to do, not just with your friends and supporters, but especially with your detractors and enemies. Looking at the world from someone else's perspective will accomplish one of two things. Either you will discover something you never realized before and perhaps come around to his or her way of thinking, or you will gain valuable insight into how to get what you want from someone you previously didn't know how to handle. Either way, you win.

When you get in the habit of looking at life from another person's point of view, you may find that you like people more, even if you don't always agree with all they say and do. When they really irritate you, you may find yourself thinking, "So-and-so is a jerk, but I still like the guy."

Wilson's Way #9: Don't Waste Valuable Time Complaining

Next to health, your time is your single most valuable possession. Some people say "time is money," and certainly, wasting time can cost you lots of cash. But there's an important difference between the two:

With effort, you have the option of making more money, but no amount of work, no matter how earnest or clever, will ever generate even one more second of time. Money may be valuable, but time is priceless.

Rich or poor, young or old, we each have the same twenty-four hours each day. How you spend your 1,440 minutes per day says more about you than how you spend your money. How you invest your 86,400 seconds per day defines your future more powerfully than how you invest your money. And while none of us knows exactly how much time we have left, we each know that life does not last forever. Therefore, every moment is infinitely precious and irreplaceable.

People who sit around, wasting their time complaining, need to get a life before its too late. Complaining is not simply nonproductive, it is counter-productive. Not only does it get you nowhere, it keeps you focused on what you *don't* want, rather than propelling you toward what you do want.

Is life hard? Yes, of course, life is hard. Is life unfair? Yes, sir, life is terribly unfair. For far too many people in this brutal world, life is inexcusably unfair. Let that motivate you into useful action, not turn you into a professional whiner. Speak up, act up, and change the world, or at least your corner of it. But dwelling on a problem without taking effective action, or hanging around with people who constantly complain about this or that—no matter how justified—is a complete waste of your precious time.

Fill you mind with better things and get to work.

<u>Wilson's Way #10: Exceed Your Own Expectations</u>

All my life I have exceeded other people's expectations. With the exception of my wonderful parents and my dear sister, who always expected the very best from me, I have encountered countless people in my life who simply assumed I had little to offer. I have also had the personal satisfaction of blazing my own path and sometimes leaving a trail of open jaws. In grammar school, I excelled when my teachers thought I couldn't. In high school, I graduated as the top male in my class when some people thought I wouldn't. Since my birth in 1936, back when colored folks rarely dreamed of becoming doctors, let alone pursued careers in academic medicine, I have defied many expectations. I dodged prejudice and intolerance at Harvard, in medical school, in the Air Force, and at nearly every turn of my professional and private life. Along the way, I like to think I helped some people get more out of themselves than they ever thought possible. And I know I have helped the University of Maryland School of Medicine discover it could go a lot further than many people thought possible.

From all these and many other life experiences, I have learned that, in addition to all the ignorance and injustice in this world, there is another powerful factor that keeps many people from reaching their full potential: It is *themselves*.

It's true that the world can be a cruel and difficult place. It's true that life is often hard and unfair. And yes, some of us do face greater obstacles than others. But absolutely none of that changes the fact that you—and only you—are the captain of your ship. Through no fault of your own, you may never get to sail the Seven Seas. But I say you have only yourself to blame if you do not get out there and paddle the heck out of your own canoe.

Hard work and stubborn persistence are absolutely essential for achieving your goals. Stick to your guns, but don't be too rigid. Be open to new ideas and the candid discussion of differing views. Throughout your career, you will continue to grow and change your mind based on the acquisition of new knowledge. In politics, some call this "flip-flopping." I call it learning.

Sometimes, after years of working towards a difficult goal and fighting for every inch of progress, it can become a habit to confront every obstacle with unwavering determination to succeed. That's great ... most of the time. But pick your battles. Sometimes, it no longer makes sense to keep plowing ahead without making headway. Know when it's time to cut your losses and move on. Win or lose, change is the one thing you can count on. Even one's successes must eventually come to an end as you begin the next chapter.

If you are a young person on the threshold of life, or if you are a mature adult considering a career change, I implore you to think seriously about a richly rewarding career in academic medicine. If you are an African American already involved in a medical career, I beg you to consider a move to academic medicine, where you are desperately needed to help promote lasting diversity in our vitally important profession.

But whatever you choose to do with your life, I ask you to find the strength to stretch yourself out and reach as far as you can go. Rather than thinking of yourself as a victim of the winds of fate, you can grab hold of what is within your control and use it to the best of your ability, expecting nothing short of the best from yourself. You deserve nothing less, and frankly, this troubled world needs all the help it can get.

If you take from me just one idea, let it be this: Stop buying into other people's definition of you! *Define yourself.* If necessary, *reinvent yourself.* You can do far more than most people think. You can do far more than you, yourself, think. Forget about your age, your weight, your race, your gender, your parents, your education, your bank account, and your track record. Forget about what you've done so far, or what you have failed to do. Forget about what "they" will say or what "they" will think. Forget them, forget me, forget the whole wide world. In fact, forget everything that has come before right now, this precious, irreplaceable moment that is unique in all of history.

Roll up your sleeves, get to work, and *impress yourself.*

Epilogue: Done at Maryland But Not Finished

On August 1, 2007, retired University of Maryland medical school dean and Vice President for Medical Affairs, Donald E. Wilson, MD, MACP, became Senior Vice President for Health Sciences at Howard University in Washington, D.C. Howard University: Prepare thyself!

Wilson received the honorary degree Doctor of Science from University of Maryland, Baltimore in 2007 and from Tufts University in 2008. In November 2008 he received the Association of American Medical Colleges most prestigious award, the Abraham Flexner award given to one whose career has had a major positive impact on medical education.

Made in the USA